D0525624

Get That Job

This is a Parragon Book
First published in 2002

Parragon
Queen Street House
4 Queen Street
Bath BA1 1HE, UK

ISBN: 0-75258-258-5

A copy of the CIP data for this book is available from the British
Library upon request.

The right of A.H. Gort to be identified as the author of this work has
been asserted in accordance with Section 77 of the Copyright,
Designs and Patents Act of 1988.

Editorial, design and layout by Essential Books, 7 Stucley Place,
London NW1 8NS

Printed and bound in China

Get That Job

A. H. Gort

p

Contents

Introduction

The world of work is changing. One of the ways it's changing is that whole new fields of expertise have grown up over the last decade and decided to call themselves 'industries'. There's the IT Industry for example. The Call Centre Industry is an all-too-familiar part of our everyday lives. In fact, the whole professional world, it seems, has decided to re-brand itself as an industry. Barbers call themselves 'The Hairdressing Industry'. PE teachers are now 'The Leisure and Fitness Industry' and even comedians call themselves 'The Comedy Industry' (I kid you not). Perhaps this is to compensate for the fact that traditional industry as we remember it is pretty much extinct.

One of the fields of expertise that is thriving in the twenty-first century is the 'Human Resources Industry'. And, like all the other new 'industries', it has developed its own jargon in order to make it appear more industrial. Where any of that jargon appears in the following pages I have tried to explain exactly what it means.

Another way the world of work has changed stems from the introduction of the 'Culture of Change'. Technological advances coupled with increased global competition means that organizations have restructured the way in which they employ people.

When you see phrases such as 'right sizing' or 'out sourcing', you can take them to mean that the old-fashioned way of employing you is a thing of the past. Long gone are the days when someone could work at the same firm for fifty years and get a nice clock at the end of the last shift.

Instead it is increasingly likely that he or she will be hired on a short-term contract or freelance basis. They'll be expected to 'multi-task' (have lots of different skills) and possibly even 'hot-desk' (use whichever space is currently available whenever they come into work). They will probably become 'non-core' members of staff. Temporary, in other words.

You'll often see advertisements for jobs that warn you in advance that you will need to be a 'positive agent for – or manager of – change'. Which pretty much means that you can expect anything to happen, and that you will need to stay flexible and adaptable to survive.

For an increasing number of us, all this change means that we are already learning how to be flexible – not just in the way we work, but in the way we look for work. We accept that we may need to have several strings to our bows in order to keep fiddling on our roof, and we have learned to live without the luxury of a 'job for life'.

But whatever kind of work we do, and however it changes, one thing remains constant. People get hired by other people. The people who do the hiring do so by making a judgement based on a mixture of the information they are given, and a gut feeling about how well the other person will do the job. They get that information and make their judgement from reading what the potential employee has written, by talking to them and by asking other people about them. And if you could sum up this whole book in a few words, that's what it would be about: developing the skills required to help you write good things about yourself, talk to people properly and make sure that they say nice things about you.

GET
ORGANIZED

Okay, this is the philosophical part out of the way straight off. If you don't like this sort of thing, you can flip straight to the next chapter. But just before you do, bear in mind that you can come back here any time if you find it's all going horribly wrong and you need a psychological boost.

There's no point misleading you here. Getting a job can be a pretty hard thing to do. Most of the time there's not enough of them to go around. And the ones that are really cool, with nice salaries, a wonderful boss and state-of-the-art canteen facilities? Well, the competition is really tough for those.

If you don't believe it's potentially difficult, then have a think about this. There are thousands of books out there on how to get a job. Hundreds of websites. Newspapers devote whole supplements to the subject. Your local high street has umpteen recruitment specialists and job counsellors up and down it. You can even watch an entire late-night cable TV channel devoted to job seeking. Everyone knows that one of the most important things you ever have to do in your life is get yourself into gainful employment. And all those experts, gurus, authors and snake-oil salesmen also know that you're going to find it so tough that you're going to be crying out for help.

The irony being that all of us are out here telling you the best way to get a job, and deep down we know that there is no 'best way' to get a job. Sure, there are loads of things you can do to improve your chances, and a whole heap of other things you shouldn't do if you want to stand a chance. I'll be pointing them out as we go along, and hopefully in such a way that I give you some kind of edge.

But the fact remains that much of what I tell you will be useless if you don't recognize the fact that you may be in for a bit of a slog here, and that you're going to have to get up every day and work full time at getting work.

Don't worry, I'm not about to launch into some self-help, stay-motivated, positive-mental-attitude rap. Quite the opposite. If you didn't want a job you wouldn't even be reading this. You'd be down at

Blockbusters picking out something to while away the time after *This Morning* has finished. So your PMA is never going to be in any doubt.

What I'll actually be doing in the first instance is bracing you for the inevitable disappointments. And in the second instance I'll be saying to you that just because you didn't get the job as fast as you'd wanted to, that doesn't mean you're rubbish. It just means that the whole looking-for-a-job thing can be a damn sight harder than anyone expected.

As far as I'm aware, no one has ever written a book called 'Waiting Around For A Job To Come Along' or 'Get Hired In Your Sleep'. Instead, they all use action verbs such as 'winning', 'hunting' and 'seeking'. And if you read the blurb on the covers, a lot of them will use the phrase 'The increasingly competitive job market'. They're telling you that a whole big bunch of people want the same job as you. So you're going to have to compete for it. And in order to do that, or to 'win', 'hunt' or 'seek' anything, you've got to be prepared. You've got to have a plan of action.

Before you even start cruising the situations vacant pages, scratching your head over your CV or polishing your best shoes, better get that plan sorted out. It's not a really big deal, and there are professionals to help if you get stuck, but if you get organized from the get-go you'll improve your chances no end. And as with so many of the areas we'll be looking at, the concept of planning is a good one, because the better you get at it, the more attractive you will become to a potential employer.

Actually, for job hunting you need two plans. A big one and a little one. The overall plan is the one that you need to keep your eye on. Call it the game plan if you like. A bit like a football manager, say. At the beginning of the season he might decide his team stands a really good shot at the European Cup. So he'll gear his preparations to that end. In the meantime, he's well aware that week-in week-out he's going to have to deliver good results in league games or else he'll be buying a copy of this book.

Your game plan is obviously to get a job. And here's

where the big planning comes in. You need to decide what kind of job you want to do. So get a piece of paper and write that down in big, bold capitals at the top. Now you'll see exactly how much help this book can be with your big plan. I have absolutely no idea what you've written. So I can't help you get that specific job. What I can do is point out a couple of tricks to help you decide what your goal is, and maybe put you in the right direction for reaching it.

If you've a very clear idea what it is that you want to do, then that's brilliant. Skip a couple of pages. If you're a little hazy on this point, then smooth out that piece of paper, suck on your pencil for a minute or two and start making a list of questions. Like so:

- What do I like doing?
- What am I good at?
- What do I hate doing?
- What am I really bad at?
- What am I trained to do?
- What can I get training to do?
- What do other people say I'm good at?

- What do I have experience at?
- What could I get experience at?
- Do I work best on my own?
- Do I work best with other people?
- Do I want to work with my brain?
- Do I want to work with my hands?
- Do I want to be in charge?
- Do I want to be told what to do?
- Do I want to earn lots of money?
- Do I want to help people?
- Do I want to work to live?
- Do I want to live to work?

There's no scoring system for answering the questions. There's no neat little psychological trick whereby you feed them all through a computer that chugs away for a couple of minutes and then spews out the answer: 'You should be a vicar.' They're just a bunch of questions that might help you think your way into working out what's right for you. You may well come across careers advice services who claim to have just such a magic formula. And by all means give them a whirl. Tick the ticky boxes and circle the appropriate digits. They may well start off a thought process that helps you come to a decision. Just be advised that in the course of writing a couple of books on the subject, I interviewed an alarming number of people who took such a test and consequently embarked on careers they either weren't suited to, or just plain hated.

On the Internet you'll find sites that promise to tell you which career you're most suited for if you just take half an hour to fill in their questionnaire. Approach with caution. At best they're gathering information so they can target market your in-box to bits. At worst you're going to get to the very last page and discover that they're asking you for a sum of money if you want to see the result. Tell them to get lost.

A list of questions on its own is not really going to help you out too much, but it should kick-start your thought processes a little if you really are undecided about your career. Here at Parragon Books, though, we reckon there is one crucial question that will be of the most help when it comes to picking your path.

It may seem obvious, but it is so easy to overlook. And here it is:

What do I really want to do ?

The reason the question is frequently overlooked is because what we really want to do is often considered fanciful or impractical – but the truth is that with some time and training, we can usually get pretty damn close to it. Remember when you were a kid and the grown-ups were always asking, 'And what do you want to be when you grow up?' I wonder how many of you said, 'I'm going to work in telesales.' Now, once again, I have no idea what you actually said, and it may be that you picked on a job that was relatively sensible – a nurse or a teacher, perhaps. In which case, you've got every chance of getting there. But for those of you who picked footballer, ballet dancer, astronaut or Red Indian, you're probably pretty much resigned to kissing your calling goodbye.

But you don't necessarily have to give up on getting

involved in those areas, now do you? Take a look at what it was that attracted you to that vocation and why you considered you'd be any good at it, and see if it doesn't lead you somewhere. You may not ever get the chance to walk out as part of the England team, for example, but there are other ways to work in football if that's what turns you on – such as coaching, groundstaff, administration or merchandising. Every football club in the land needs employees. The same thing goes for dance companies. There's even a troupe of enthusiasts touring the country re-enacting Wild West battles. And they're getting paid for it. They might need Red Indians! In Dukinfield – a scruffy little town in Cheshire – there's a bloke called Steve Bennett who always wanted to be an astronaut. So he started building his own rockets. And they go into space. And his next project is to raise enough money through sponsorship to enable him to get inside one and go up with it.

Deep down in your heart of hearts you know what it is you really want to do. So write it down.

GET REAL Gary always wanted to be a train driver. In his teens he even 'acquired' a train driver's uniform and used to ride up and down the country teaching himself the routes. At college he took a course in photography, mainly in order to improve the pictures he took of trains. Then for ten years he ran his own photo-processing lab, which gave him ulcers and made him miserable. So he quit and took a fairly low-paid job working on the information desk for a rail company. His plan is to learn the ropes and apply to take the tests to become a train driver.

Obviously, with the benefit of a grown-up perspective you'll know how realistic your goal is and what sort of compromises you may have to make. But remember that this is your long-term plan – your 'European Cup'. So at this first attempt you can be as ambitious as you like.

Once again I'm hampered by not being able to see what you've written. So for the purposes of showing you the next bit of planning, bear with me and let me imagine that you have actually written 'vicar' as your idea of an ideal job.

Okay. What you need to do now is figure out how you make your dream happen. Have a bit of a suck on your pencil again, and then underneath 'vicar' make some more notes. Like so:

- Get GCSE Religion
- Do theology degree
- Practise reading Bible out loud
- Learn how to organize a jumble sale
- Meet a bishop
- Read situations vacant page in *Vicars & Vergers Weekly*

Many apologies to any real vicars who may be reading this (and to those who are – sorry the vicaring isn't working out). It must be apparent that I have absolutely no idea whatsoever about how one goes about becoming a man of the cloth. However, that's not really the point of the exercise. The point is that you need to have a good plan of action to enable you to achieve your ambition. And whatever your chosen field, you need to be able to find out how you can get there. That should be relatively easy. Many books offer specialist advice in specific fields, and careers guidance counsellors are available all over the place to give you a helping hand.

But absolutely the best way to learn about becoming a vicar is to ask a vicar. Preferably, ask a couple of them. In other words, go directly to the person who does the job you really want to do, and say 'How did you get there?' There are three significant advantages to getting the information you need from a real live practitioner of the profession you wish to follow, and they are as follows:

1. Obviously they did it, so they know one of the ways to do it. Talk to two or three people and you may well get two or three tried-and-tested methods of getting into your chosen profession.

2. You'll also get an insight into the job that no book or dispassionate third party can give you. That includes the downsides. Hidden snags that only someone in the job knows. Sacrifices that may have to be made, for example. Or shifting work patterns that render third-party information out of date.

3. Perhaps most importantly, you'll be making useful contacts in the trade. As you'll see as you read on, that's one of the things we believe is most vital to looking for a job. Who knows where those contacts will lead? Not only do they know about the job, but they know about The Jobs. We'll be coming back to this later.

It may well be that you have to revise that second list a little after you've done your research; you may even have a couple of optional things on the list. But you will have a list and, broadly speaking, it will encompass the following:

> Training
> Experience
> Contacts
> Research

All of these areas will be covered in detail in the following pages, but for now you've hopefully got something approaching a big plan. And that's a good thing to have. At this point, however, I should sound a cautionary note. And that is: don't get too hung up on the plan. What you absolutely, positively don't want to end up with here is a 'von Schlieffen Plan'.

General von Schlieffen was responsible for the plan that mobilized the German army prior to the First World War. He drew up a complex scheme to move troops in huge numbers at lightning speed, utilizing the advanced rail network. Even though he was dead when the rumblings of war started, his plan was executed with impressive results in 1914. One and a half million troops were moved to the French and Belgian borders in a matter of weeks; up to five hundred trains a day were deployed. The only problem was that he'd never built into his plan a contingency to actually stop the war machine. It quickly became apparent to the German high command that it was pointless attending any more peace talks. Even with the best will in the world they couldn't deviate from the plan. They were going to start a whole world war, come what may.

What we're saying is that any written-down plan is only a guide to the way you conduct your campaign. You will need some flexibility so that you can respond to any new opportunities that may arise. It would also be really rotten if you ended up in some career that you really hated – and we all know people who have – just because you stuck too rigidly to a career plan.

Paradoxically perhaps, the second bunch of planning should be adhered to with some rigidity. That's because it's your day-to-day action plan that is going to really get you the job. All we're talking about here is some basic administration. One file. One notepad. One pencil to suck on the end of, and some time set aside each day to suck on it.

The file is to keep a record of all job applications, advertisements you see, copies of all correspondence and as much information as you can gather on each company you think you might want to work for.

The notebook is to make a daily list of all the calls you need to make, the letters you need to write, the e-mails you should send, the newspapers you should read and any research you need to do. We're not going to say a whole lot about the subject of administration here, except that it is possibly one of the most vital – and frequently overlooked – aspects of your job searching. For three good reasons:

- It gives you an edge over all those muppets who think that administering a job search means occasionally glancing at the 'positions' page of *Vicars & Vergers Weekly*.
- If you are out of work it gives you a structure to work within and helps you to maintain good working practices.
- Good administration skills are always in demand by employers.

If possible, you might like to think about making a space for yourself at home that is like an 'office'. Nothing fancy. Just a chair and table by the phone will do. That way you can concentrate on the job of getting a job in a set place at a set time, and it will almost be like going to work each day. And it does really need to be each day. One of the most common pitfalls that job

GET IN TOUCH There's no shortage of careers advice all over the place these days. And like any kind of advice it can range from rubbish to indifferent. Even advice that you have to pay for can be iffy, so best to think twice before you go down that road. There are two places to go to find where the nearest good, free advice to you is. First off is your local Job Centre. They know what you're entitled to, and who's dishing it out. The second place is www.careers.co.uk. It's a nifty little site that allows you to access all sorts of government-accredited outfits in your town.

seekers fall into is to start off with commendable zeal and enthusiasm for the first couple of days – weeks even – then, when the going gets tough, they get a comfy position on the sofa from which they can watch daytime TV. We cannot stress enough that finding a job, particularly the right job, can be a long process with not a lot to show for it in the early stages. So the daily plan has to be stuck to on a long-term basis.

Just one more bit of philosophical stuff before we get on to the practical side. Don't take it so personally when you don't get hired. First off, job hunting is like any other skill: it takes time to develop. You'll get better at all aspects the more you do it. So expect to screw it up occasionally, just learn from your experience and push on regardless. Second, it's fair to say that the people who do the recruiting often don't have anything like the resources that you do to help them. There are very few books and websites entitled 'Get That Ideal Employee'. Which means that they probably just failed to recognize how marvellous you are. If you don't believe us then look at some of the halfwits who are employed that you deal with on a daily basis.

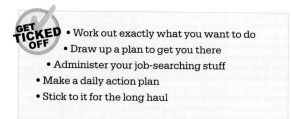

GET TICKED OFF

- Work out exactly what you want to do
- Draw up a plan to get you there
- Administer your job-searching stuff
- Make a daily action plan
- Stick to it for the long haul

GET SOME
TRAINING

Solely for the purposes of giving us some sort of illustrative career path, let's continue in the rest of the book assuming that you've decided to become a vicar. Obviously you haven't, but here's my inspiration: I was staring out the window thinking of the best way to make my point and the vicar walked past. Could've been a whole lot worse. I live not too far away from a red-light district.

Okay. So whatever it is – vicar, tart or structural engineer – you must accept that before you can apply for a job you have to be able to do the job. You have to be convinced of that fact. And the prospective employer has to be even more convinced. The two most effective ways to prove you can do it are to show that you have already done it, or wave a piece of official-looking paper under his or her nose that says, in the case of our would-be vicar, 'This candidate is dead good at praying.'

'On-the-job training' is a whole lot easier in some professions than in others. You would imagine that for a structural engineer a grasp of mathematics, architecture and wolf-whistling would be crucial long before they allowed you on site to muck about with girders. But in a lot of instances there are routes that you can go down both to acquire skills and find out how you like the job. One such way is to go in at 'entry level' and ensure that you've picked an outfit that appreciates the value of investing in staff training. In other words, if you're a prospective structural engineer approach the engineering company, explain that you've always fancied building bridges but are prepared to initially work sweeping up and making tea for minimum wage provided there are opportunities to advance your career. This works for both you and the employer. They get to suss out how hard working and dedicated you are, and – aside from the obvious training benefits – you get to find out if you're suited to the job.

Similar benefits can be derived from volunteering. In fact, a whole load of benefits can ensue from pursuing this course. If you pitch up at the engineering company and say, 'I've always fancied being a structural engineer, do you think I could work for you on a voluntary basis – one day a week maybe – for a month or so? See how I get on', I bet you very quickly get a taker. This is actually one of the most effective ways of job seeking we know. Think about it. Employers get really up-tight about hiring new staff. It's a real pain in the neck going through all that recruiting and selection process. They worry big time that they might end up handing over a valuable position to a complete schmuck.

That's why they tend to employ people they know, or who are known by people they know. If you work there for a while and prove yourself to be a sedulous and trustworthy worker, they'll soon recognize that fact. Even if they have nothing immediately, you'll be top of the list when anything does come in. Obviously you shouldn't let them exploit you – put a time limit on the length of free time you give each potential employer – but this is as close as you're going to get to a guaranteed job-finding method.

The other way to exploit any free time you may

GET IN TOUCH Pretty much every town in the UK has a volunteer bureau. Their job is to give you information and advice on what's available locally. So swing by there at some point. Or check out the pages on volunteering at www.thesite.org. They have a very nifty search engine that allows you to select the stuff you're interested in and match you up with the nearest organization doing that stuff.

have is to join up as a volunteer for a bona fide voluntary organization. The opportunities here are practically endless, and the benefits manifold. If you're looking for your very first job, for example, this really is the best way to get some useful stuff on your CV. You can pick something you're really, really interested in. Most voluntary organizations offer their workers excellent free training facilities.

The more traditional way to get trained is to go on

some sort of course. Hereabouts it gets potentially bewildering. There are thousands of the things. Hundreds of qualifications and dozens of places to learn.

To pick the right one for you, you're best advised to go and talk to some people. Specifically, the people who are doing the job you want to get trained for. So, to return once more to our ecclesiastical example, grab the vicar and pump him. You want to know which courses he went on, whether they were worthwhile and whether he knows what's available currently. You also want to get down to the Job Centre and local employment advice bodies and check out what's happening in your locale.

Before you take up any kind of training or additional learning you also need to evaluate exactly what it's going to cost you. Getting an education can be an expensive business, so get that area researched thoroughly. And don't forget that there's more to it than just the course fees. Books and equipment will all add to the expense. But you need to think of more than just the financial investment. You are going to need to put in time and energy as well. Even a part-time course can be

GET LOST

Even in the world of further education there are some scoundrels out there. The last thing you want is to invest time, energy and money in attending some half-baked sessions with a half-hearted halfwit who only knows half the story. You won't half be sorry. Hang around outside the place and accost some of the students as they leave. They'll give you the lowdown. If you attend an interview or enrolment session, ask if you can talk to a few people who completed the course. If you get fobbed off, alarm bells should start ringing right then and there.

quite demanding. Not only will there be classes to attend but there may well be additional course work, reading, essays and assignments to deal with. So make sure you know everything that's entailed before you commit yourself. You won't learn much if you're exhausted all the time.

If you're unemployed at the moment, then a whole lot of learning should be available to you free of charge. Just be aware that studying for more than sixteen hours a week may affect your benefits. If in doubt, ask an advisor at your Job Centre. Given that the training you have plumped for will be for the specific purpose of taking you off the dole, they will be super helpful. If you're not in receipt of benefits then you should check out this number:

LEARN DIRECT: 0800 100 900

This is a hotline run by the Department of Education and Employment. Not only are they dead helpful at steering you in the right direction of good accredited courses, but they'll advise you on the best way of funding your studies. They even offer their members excellent discounts on certain kinds of courses.

As you probably know, the days of the full student grant are pretty much gone for ever. There are some funding sources still available, however, and there's an

Educational Grants Advisory Centre that you can contact if you want to explore this option. They're at 501/505 Kingsland Road, London E8 4AU.

In most cases, though, you'll be looking at some kind of loan if you want to engage in full-time education. The best option is the Career Development Loan scheme. Basically, the money comes from the government and is administered by some of the high-street banks. Anyone can apply, but you need to be able to convince a bank manager that at the end of the training you'll get a job that enables you to repay the loan. And obviously, you can't just spend the money on sweeties. It's supposed to cover course fees and materials and to contribute to your living expenses. The advantage of a CDL is that the government meets the interest payments during the studying period and for a while afterwards. You also don't have to start paying it back until you start work. The amount you pay back is geared to your salary, so that you shouldn't ever have to suffer too much hardship. Once again the full details are available from Learn Direct.

There is one single area of training that if you haven't got, you should put this book right down now and get sorted out. That's IT. Information Technology. Computers. If we haven't yet reached the time where it's impossible to get and keep a job without knowing how to use them, then we're pretty damn close.

As we'll see later on, a computer is also pretty vital to your job-hunting endeavours, so there can be no hiding place. Time to get to grips with the beast in the machine. Free training for Information Technology is just about the most bountiful form of learning there is. A really good place to start would be your local library – if they don't have a learning centre there, and the majority do, they will have information on where the nearest one to you is.

Don't get too hung up on these boxes of plastic junk full of strange initials and vaguely smutty-sounding error messages. Provided you don't lose your rag and chuck one out of the window (admittedly a very real possibility at times) they are virtually indestructible and, approached systematically, very

GET REAL

Ed had been off work sick for some years. He was keen to get back into employment, but nervous about entering the full-time job market. He also had no computer experience whatsoever.

Ed kept birds of prey as a hobby and had heard of an excellent website all about kestrels. It was his interest in the birds that drove him to enrol on a course at his local library called 'Computing For The Terrified'. Within a matter of days he was whizzing about the World Wide Web as if he owned it.

In the course of his studies he noticed that all the suppliers of falconry gauntlets were some way away from his home. Ed had been making his own gauntlets for years, so he approached local retailers, discovered that there was a demand for the gloves and started supplying them. Through those contacts he also managed to get work as a freelance falconry expert.

simple to use. You don't even have to be any good at typing. Which is just as well. Because this entire book (and a couple of others) was written on a computer by someone who types like a one-eyed monkey.

To give you an idea of the types of courses and training available, along with what's entailed, here's a bit of a rundown:

Evening classes

Your nearest college or learning centre will run all manner of courses and you're usually only committed to a couple of hours per week. You'll find that many of them cross the line from esoteric to absurd – and if Tai Chi Basket Folding is vital to your career, then go for it – but practically speaking you should be able to study any academic subject up to GCSE A Level. This is also one of the best places to go if you feel that you need some help with what are called 'Essential Skills' – those fairly basic things that you feel may be holding you back, perhaps just because it's been a while since you were at school. We're talking about literacy, numeracy, spelling, grammar etc. These days, the use of computers is also considered an 'Essential Skill'. Once again the local library is the first stop in accessing information on when and where these classes are.

WEA classes

The Workers' Educational Association is fundamentally a long-established philanthropic organization. The main thrust of their approach is to make education available to those who wouldn't normally have access to it. They also place more emphasis on personal development than academic qualifications. But don't let that put you off – their courses are very reasonably priced and taught by qualified experts. Incidentally, if you have qualifications or experience yourself that may be of use to others then you might consider registering with the WEA as a tutor. The money is good and the range of subjects wide. For learning or teaching opportunities, the nearest WEA centre to you is in the phone book.

Access courses

This is an excellent way to get educated if you've been out of the game for a while, or never had any specific further education. You have to be over 21 and prepared to commit some time and effort, but the courses are designed to be flexible so that you can work the rest of your life around them. Pretty much any subject is available and many of the learning centres are hooked up to a university, enabling students easier access to a subsequent degree course. Those nice people at Learn Direct on 0800 100 900 will give you the full lowdown.

Distance learning

The best known of the distance learning outfits is the Open University. If your perception of that is kipper-tied boffins mumbling incoherently on TV at four in the a.m., forget about it. Both the OU and many of the other schemes now running have upgraded to exciting and sophisticated courses with all that you need to get educated, challenged and qualified. There's no age limit, no need for entry qualifications and best of all you can study at your own pace and in your own time. You get your own personal tutor to guide you through each stage, and many of the courses will have the option for you to attend local study centres for tutorials and lectures, so that you don't feel too isolated. If you fancy the distance learning option and believe that you have the self-motivation required, then hit the phone and get the lowdown off the Learn Direct Helpline.

Vocational qualifications

You may have to wade through a whole heap of initials to get to grips with whichever is the best one for you. GNVQ, NVQ and HND for example. Basically, the gist of them all is that they put more emphasis on what you can do as opposed to getting a piece of paper to declare what you might be able to do. Although there may well be some classwork involved in a vocational qualification, the bulk of them will concentrate on specific career-related training. Consequently they are the favourite route for switched-on, training-conscious employers keen to get their staff up to scratch. So if you're in employment, talk to your firm about the possibilities, which may well include some form of day release to study at a local college. NVQ (National Vocational Qualification) and GNVQ (the same, but with General in front of it) courses run at all sorts of levels. They cover every form of practical training and are available from every kind of learning centre. In a lot of cases they can even be used as entry qualifications to get you onto a degree course. You know the drill by now. Phone Learn Direct.

New Deal

One of the things that governments hate most is people being out of work for long periods. So if that's you, the government hates you (don't worry, I'm sure it's mutual). Consequently, every now and again they are going to come up with some innovative initiative that's designed to return you to the ranks of the useful tax payer. At the time of writing, that's the New Deal. The thinking behind it is that people with no work experience find getting work a difficult experience. So the government will do a deal with you. And this is it. They'll carry on paying your dole, and you'll do as you're told. First off you'll be appointed a Personal Advisor who will work out with you what type of work you might be able to do. If you're under 25 you'll then get to go on a 'Gateway' course, in which you'll cover pretty much the kind of stuff you'll read in this book. If being personally advised and gatewayed doesn't lead to a job, then the likeliest outcome is that they'll find you a job and pay the employer a subsidy towards your wages. But one of the options considered is that of full-time training or education. The whole thing is administered from your Job Centre, and the advisors therein will be keen to get you off their hands as soon as possible, so watch out for the ones that may just see you as a way of meeting their targets.

Whatever form of training you choose to take – and we do hope you seriously consider it – there is a ton of help and experience to put you on the right track. So much so, it can boggle the mind, even before you've actually sat down and started studying. So we would like to reiterate the advice we gave at the beginning (and will continue to give). Talk to people who do the job you want to do. They'll know the best course to take, even if it's through the rotten experience of having taken the wrong one themselves.

GET TICKED OFF

- Consider volunteering for a job you fancy
- Talk to people who already do the job you want to do
- Work out exactly what you need to commit to a course in terms of both time and money
- Call the Learn Direct Helpline on 0800 100 900 for brilliant advice
- Prioritize acquiring and improving your Information Technology skills

GET THAT JOB BEFORE **A**NYONE ELSE

Think like a job hunter. Think a little like your prey – the employer you're going to track down. What do they want? Well, they don't particularly want to have to go looking for you if they can help it. Putting ads in the paper, dealing with all those applications, selections and rejections is all well and good if you're a huge company with a dedicated personnel department. But for most employers, the ideal way to hire people is to have the perfect candidate just drop magically out of the sky.

So all you have to do is learn how to drop magically out of the sky. Aside from making you appear like manna from heaven to a prospective boss, this approach will put you way ahead of all the other sluggards who are still diligently buying a paper once a week and keeping their fingers crossed.

And how exactly do you achieve this feat of fantastical free fall? Here's an acronymic mnemonic to help you out:

- Research
- Usurp
- Network

In other words, RUN for that job. Let's suppose that you're still hellbent on a career as a vicar. Buying *Vicars & Vergers Weekly* may well be a smart thing to do, but by the time it appears any jobs advertised therein will have been available for some time. If, on the other hand, you'd bought the *News of the World* some weeks earlier, you may have seen an item telling you that the vicar of Chipping-Sodbury-On-Sea had run off with an actress. That would tell you that there was most likely to be a vacancy coming up in that particular parish, thereby giving you an opportunity to get ahead of the pack. You would have done some research.

The opportunities for researching your job hunt are manifold and once you get into it, you'll discover more and more ways to find stuff out about what jobs may be coming available. And like many of the skills we're looking at in this chapter (and in chapters to come), you'll be twice blessed if you deploy it. In common recruitment parlance, it is what they call a 'transferable skill'. In other words, something that you have learnt to do in one aspect of your life that you can also do in your professional life. When it comes to writing your CV you can confidently put 'excellent researcher' down as one of your key personal strengths.

Probably one of the most useful areas for researching potential vacancies is your local media. The more local the better. It's there that you'll find all manner of information indicating who is likely to be hiring staff. Your local papers carry details of planning applications, new developments, government initiatives, personnel changes, profit announcements and heaps of other useful stuff. Some of them even tell you when people are retiring or leaving a job to go work some other place. All of these will give you a varying degree of advanced knowledge about what kind of vacancies are likely to be coming up. Once you've studied them for a while they'll also tell you about what the recruitment jargonistas refer to as 'employment trends'. In other words, what kind of business is on the increase in your area. That could give you a clue as to what kind of training you should be considering.

These days your library is also a mine of information on what's happening with local businesses and employment trends. Ask the librarians. They're roughly divided into two groups. Avoid the first group who just tut and look at you like you deserve to be out of work. Go for the second – happily more prevalent – lot, who will bend over backwards to show you how to source the information you need.

While we'll be dealing with the World Wide Web in more detail later on, it's worth a mention here. Even quite small companies have their own websites these days. Practically all larger companies do. Not only will these give you invaluable background on the organization you're interested in, but many of them will carry details of vacancies before they ever appear in any newspaper.

Keep your eyes open as you walk around too. No matter how short a walk it might be to your local shop, the chances are that you will pass umpteen clues as to what kind of vacancies are available. For example, every time they clear a piece of land for development these days, pretty much the first thing they do is put up a whacking great sign. The sign will tell you what they're building, when it's likely to be finished and frequently carries contact details.

Across the road from me (next door to the church) is an engineering workshop called, improbably, 'Impregnation Services Ltd.' Obviously I have asked about getting involved in research and development, but it turns out they deal in a whole other kind of impregnation. For the last three years they appear to have employed two big blokes and a singularly ugly cat to do a lot of standing around scratching their crotches. But just lately I've become acutely aware of – and annoyed by – a constant procession of huge trucks coming and going at all hours of the day and night. There's more blokes too. And a lot less crotch scratching. Even for the cat. This would perhaps indicate that there are job opportunities for the asking.

And don't make the mistake of thinking that just because they're an impregnation service all they'll be looking for is impregnators. As they grow, their infrastructure will develop. They may well need accounts people, caterers, drivers, sales staff, extra mousers. All manner of positions could be available.

That's just one small example, obviously. But if you decide to spend a week being a full-time 'hidden vacancy' (a bit more recruitment jargon for you there) researcher, you'll so quickly get into the swing of it that by the second week it will become almost second nature to you.

Your research shouldn't stop with finding the hidden vacancies, by the way. Should you secure an interview at any place through any means, that's when it really kicks in. The more you can find out about any prospective employer, the better it is. For two reasons. One is that it gives you a real edge when it comes to selection. They'll be dead impressed that you know so much about them, they may even believe that you really, really want to work there. Second of all, you're doing yourself a big favour. Objective research is going to give you the best clue as to whether or not you really want to work there.

This guy Micah, who drinks in the same bar as me, told me about a guy he knew who used to go to job interviews and challenge the interviewers to ask him any question about their firm. Such was the quality of his research, he was evidently never caught out. He also used to bet that he could tell them things about their own company that they didn't even know. Now quite

GET IN TOUCH Pretty much every town now has a TEC or Training Enterprise Centre (in Scotland they're called Local Enterprise Centres). If you're looking for work, these are good places to track down for a whole load of reasons, not least of which being that they produce all sorts of literature to help you improve some of the skills we've gone into in this chapter, along with workshops and training sessions. Sometimes they have different names from TEC, so ask at your local Job Centre where the nearest one to you is.

frankly he sounds like an annoying know-it-all, but there's something to be said for doing that level of research, without necessarily going to the point of using it to patronize – and potentially irritate – the would-be employer.

Of course, it's pointless running around town doing all this impressive research, and then just sitting at home gloating about it. You need to develop a strategy to put it to use. You need to get in there before the schmucks who read the paper once a week hear about the job. You need to usurp their asses. Primarily by making sure that the potential employer knows about you before he knows about anyone else.

There are three basic ways to go about registering your interest:

• Phone them up
• Write to them
• Call in person

All of these are perhaps going to take some chutzpah you didn't know you had, but like everything else, once you've done it a few times, you'll be in a whole new skill-learning world. Another one that will stand you in good stead when it comes to being employable. Someone who in the first instance shows initiative and in the second instance has the cojones to follow through is exactly what most employers are looking for.

Let's deal with the first one first, then. It's probably the most straightforward – in so far as you need a telephone, a notebook or file and the ubiquitous pencil to write things down with and suck the end of. Obviously you'll need some phone numbers too, but you should have researched these by now. You'll also need to know who to speak to. If your research hasn't specifically unearthed you the right contact, then the best thing to do is to make a preliminary call to the company to find out. To a large extent, the size of the organization will dictate how far up the chain of command you get to reach.

Larger outfits will have a dedicated personnel department that exists solely to find the best people to hire. They'll probably be professional enough to have a system in place for dealing with the likes of you, and you'd be best advised just making a good impression and making sure that you comply with their procedure. I suspect, on the other hand, that if you fancied working at Impregnation Services Ltd. right now, it's still small enough for the owner or managing director to be in charge of hiring and firing.

Once you've established exactly who you need to be talking to, then you need to make that call. Have a bit of a think about exactly what you're going to say beforehand. You might even want to jot down a few rough notes to give you a guideline. It's probably best not to write it all out as a script, though. You might end up sounding like one of those annoying people that ring you all the time trying to sell you stuff you don't really want.

When you call, make sure that you've got peace and quiet around you – no TV blaring or flying crockery noises. It's time to focus entirely on the person you're going to be speaking to. Take into consideration that they're likely to be busy people, promise that you're only going to keep them for a couple of minutes, and stick to that promise. Let's suppose that you're still keen on that job as a vicar at St Cuthbert's and you've found out that the person responsible for hiring vicars is Bishop Van Hessen. Your conversation might go something like this:

Him: *Hello, Bishop Van Hessen speaking. How can I help you?*

You: *Oh, hello your Bishopness, my name is Havelock Dayne and I won't keep you a minute. I understand that there may soon be a vacancy at St Cuthbert's. I am a fully trained vicar with a good knowledge of the area, and I wondered how I might go about applying for the position.*

Him: *Well, Mr Dayne, we won't be interviewing for a couple of weeks yet, but if you could send your CV to my secretary, we'll certainly keep it on file.*

You: *I shall do that very thing. Are there any particular requirements that I would need for this position?*

Him: *Well, we are looking for someone with vast experience of organizing jumble sales.*

You: *Oh that's good, jumble sales are one of my areas of expertise. Thank you so much for your time and trouble. I shall drop my CV in later today. Goodbye.*

In real life, of course, things don't always go that swimmingly well, but the above example should give you a rough idea of the kind of things you need to say. Notice that while you kept the bishop for just the minute you promised, you did manage to winkle out one piece of important information – the bit about the jumble sales. By so doing, you were also able to make the point that this is one of your strong areas. You can make sure that you reiterate that in your CV and covering letter.

Notice also that you promised to 'drop my CV in later'. If that's feasible, then you should do it. While some employers wait until they have all the applications in before starting their selection process, others will start as soon as they get them. So the earlier a bird you are, the juicier the worms you might get. Plus, if you do live locally and are able to drop your CV in by hand, then you might get to speak to the bishop in person. You'll certainly get to see his secretary, who might be another source of information on the job. They could possibly even be on the selection panel.

If you decide to write a letter, then you should also keep it as brief as possible. No more than a couple of paragraphs should do the trick. You should certainly never run to over a page. People who get a lot of mail tend to glance quickly at the first page to see if it is of any interest to them. If it looks long, tedious and largely irrelevant, it will get binned. The body of your letter may look something like this:

Dear Bishop Van Hessen,

I understand that you may shortly have a vacancy for a vicar at St Cuthbert's Church. I would be delighted if you would consider my application for the job. I have enclosed my CV and as you can see I passed my third-year Vicaring GNVQ with honours. I also have vast experience of organizing jumble sales and have recently started helping out the vicar at St Marmalade's on a voluntary basis.

I wonder if it might be possible to have a chat with you at some point about exactly what kind of experience and qualifications you are looking for. Perhaps I could telephone later this week to make an appointment to come and see you.

Yours etc.

By all means enclose your CV, but don't necessarily expect it to get read in detail. That's why it's a good idea in any covering letter to punch up the key points, without rambling on and on until the letter is as long as your CV. In the letter above, notice the fact that you made a definite statement about how you were going to contact the bishop. Give it a week or so and then make that follow-up call. It shows that you are keen and interested – and don't ever be shy about showing how keen and interested you are in a job vacancy.

Provided you really are, that is something that will attract an employer: people who really, really, really want to work for them.

The third way to make contact is to swing by and see if you can have a chat. Once again, you need to take into consideration just how busy people are, so if you promise to take 'just two minutes' then make sure you do exactly that. The chances are that they will be so busy that they can't see you at such short notice, so the beauty of this method is that you can stand there and get an appointment. And if it's a receptionist, secretary or assistant that you deal with, be just as polite and interested as you would be if it were the head honcho. Who knows, you may have to work with these people some day. And if you're snotty or dismissive, they will tell the boss.

If it all sounds a little daunting, don't worry too much about it. It doesn't even matter if you screw up the first couple of times. Just come away from the experience, have a good think about where you went wrong, and try to put it right next time.

GET REAL Mike was fed up working in local government. He'd been doing it so long he was finding it boring and predictable. He liked hanging around in bars, though. He found them interesting and unpredictable. Some places he'd been hanging around in so much, he'd become friendly with the owners. So he started asking if he could help out behind the bar at weekends and in the evenings. Gradually he increased his hours behind bars and eventually gave up his job at the council to manage a very big and prestigious city centre venue.

It may also be that you decide that you are stronger in one area of approach than another, and should concentrate more on that. If I'm looking for work, for example, I am more confident of writing a good letter than anything else. When you're as big and ugly as I am, you tend to come across better on paper than you do in person.

The last and most useful part of our RUN mnemonic is Networking. And all that means is talking to people. Initially, people you know. Think about it. If you know ten people with jobs, that means you have ten contacts who might know if there's a job coming up at their place. And if they're people you know really well, then that's ten people who might be able to put in a good word for you if a vacancy becomes available.

No matter how 'fair and impartial' a recruitment policy is supposed to be, the truth is that most employers like to employ someone they know they can rely on. The next best thing is to employ someone who someone else they know tells them they can rely on. So keep on asking everyone you know. Don't become a total pain, but a gentle reminder every now and again will keep you fresh in their minds. Just remember to buy them dinner if they get you a result.

You should also try talking to people you don't know. Find out who works at the place you want to work at and see if you can't get to know them a little better. Be upfront about it, by all means. Let them know that you are really interested in their work because you fancy moving into that field yourself. If you get short shrift, then accept that some people might be defensive about their position, and move on to someone else. But if you're polite, diplomatic and enthusiastic, you might make a valuable friend and contact. You'll also get to find out all the stuff that they don't tell you in the job adverts. So you're not just networking, you're researching at the same time.

All of the above will take some effort and – if you set about it right – some discipline, but the rewards will make it worthwhile. Not only do you stand a much better chance of getting a job, but you will improve on some key skills that will make you a much more attractive employee. You'll also appear to a prospective boss as if you just dropped magically out of the sky. So the chances are that they will like you just that bit more than if they'd had to spend precious time and money looking for you.

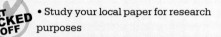

- Study your local paper for research purposes
- Walk around with your eyes open, looking for job opportunities
- Get to the jobs before they're advertised
- Be polite with every potential new contact
- Make sure all your friends and family know you are looking for work

GET ONLINE

If you're not webbed up yet, then now is the time to look into it. The Internet is a fantastic job-hunting tool and is likely to become increasingly important in all of our future careers. Not only can you look for jobs online, but you can apply for them – faster than anyone else. You can get career advice – both general and specific to the career you chose – and as a research tool, it's second to none.

I could write the whole book here about the Internet and how it works and what opportunities there are for job seekers. Well, I couldn't. But someone clever could. And lots of people have. So if you're new to the whole world of webness, then it's probably best to get yourself one of those books. The one I found most useful when I was starting out was *The Guardian Guide to the Internet* by a bloke called Jim McClellan. It was only £5.99, it explains everything very clearly and – I thought this was important – it's small enough to fit between your keyboard and your computer while you work. While I'm at it, it's also worth checking out two recently published Parragon Books titles –

GET REAL Louise was a librarian. She quite enjoyed her job, but fancied doing something a little more challenging. The library where she worked was quite progressive, and was consequently one of the first to get online. Louise was intrigued by the World Wide Web and recognized very early on its power as a research tool. She soon became proficient in all aspects of Internet use and in her spare time took courses on web design. Using her newly acquired skills and online contacts, she landed herself a job as a full-time web designer and consultant. She now makes great big piles of money, which she spends mainly on shoes. Because she likes shoes.

Understanding the Internet and *Understanding Your PC* – both of which are concise and informative aids to getting to grips with the kind of technology you'll have to be familiar with in today's employment market.

If you have a computer at home then these books will be a big help in ensuring that you have the right equipment and advice to get online. Don't worry if you have neither the space nor, more crucially, the money to get a home PC – there are other options available to you. The library is probably the best amongst them. Not only are libraries pretty much all online these days, they are very cheap to use and, crucially, there are lots of lovely librarians to help you get started and sort out any problems you may have.

Another option is to try a high-street Internet café. They are all over the place now and, of course, they have the advantage that you can surf the Web, slurp a latte and munch on an exciting cake at the same time. They can be a bit pricey, however, particularly once you've factored in the cost of that fancy cake. And sometimes the staff can be a little too busy at best – or too inexperienced at worst – to spare the time to help out an absolute beginner.

Once you've logged on, the very first thing you should suss out is your e-mail account. This is your electronic post office, allowing you to send and receive mail, documents, pictures and sounds at the push of a couple of buttons. You'll get your own address, which looks something like this: sandy-gort@elvis.com. That's mine, feel free to e-mail me with offers of work, invitations to long lunches and reasonably priced Elvis memorabilia. At the time of writing, the majority of e-mail services are free. Once you have registered, you can also access your account with a password from any computer.

An e-mail account is vital to your job hunting, primarily because it is the single fastest way to contact people. It's also the cheapest. So, specifically for jobs in other parts of the country – or overseas – you can't beat it. There are a couple of things to be wary of, however. Never rely on it totally as a way of contacting people. Particularly busy people who run large departments. They get dozens, sometimes hundreds of e-mails every working week, and there is a tendency for some folk to run through them, deleting any that look as if they're not important. If you've e-mailed a prospective employer and you don't hear anything after a couple of days, it's best to play safe by following up with a letter or phone call.

With that in mind it's a good idea to be as brief as possible when using the medium of electronic mail. And although you don't have to lay out an e-mail as you do a letter, it's best to follow the protocol of being polite and formal. Buck the trend of using smiley icons and abbreviated terms when writing within the context of a job application. And watch your spelling very closely. While a lot of e-mail services carry a spell-checking facility, many don't. And even those that do aren't anywhere near as effective as those within normal word-processing programs.

The thing to remember about typing an e-mail while connected to the Internet is that the program you are using is not as powerful as the one you use for normal word processing. For that reason it's also not a good idea to type or paste your CV directly into your covering message. It looks rubbish when it turns up at the other end. In some cases, the two e-mail programs may be incompatible, which means it will just look like a series of symbols and letters. If you are sending your CV, work out how to use the 'attachments' facility. If your e-mail account doesn't work with attachments, then switch to one that does.

There is something about using an instantaneous medium that sometimes causes people's blood to rush to their heads. So never send an e-mail without printing it off first. Have a good look at it, check it for mistakes and ask yourself if you are sure that it gives the right impression about you. One last word of warning. My Internet guru – who is called Piers – once told me, 'Remember, an e-mail is as personal and private as a postcard.' This is particularly true of any that you send to large companies, some of which even employ security staff to monitor what is being sent via their computers. So if you think that blackmail, bribery or the offer of sexual favours is going to get you a job, don't use e-mail to make the point.

Once your e-mail account is up and running – and you've tested it out by firing a couple off to some mates and asking them to respond – it's time to explore the research capabilities of the World Wide Web. You now have the power to find out pretty much anything about any company or subject. There are literally billions of pages of information available to you, and at first sight it can be daunting and bewildering. As this information isn't catalogued into any specific order, you need to learn how to use 'search engines'. I'm not going to tell you how to do that. You're going to have to read a book or ask a librarian. With minimal tuition and a little bit of practice you will quickly get the hang of narrowing down your search so that you don't spend hours at sites that are of no benefit to you.

Here's another word of warning. Given that you have all these billions of pages to look at, and a whole heap of them will appear to be useful when it comes to finding yourself a job, keep a close eye on how much time you spend online looking for work. Remember that the Internet is just one of the areas that you should be looking at. It's probably best to allocate a set period each day or week to searching the

Web so that you don't neglect the other aspects of your job search.

For specifically finding out about a company or field that you want to work in, the Internet is invaluable to you. A company or organization often has its own site, for a start. That will give you their official line on what it is they do and how they do it. It will also carry details of contacts, and in a lot of cases tell you about any forthcoming vacancies and give instructions on how to apply. As in all applications for jobs, it's best to comply with those instructions. Any deviation from the standard usually results in the binning of the application. And Internet binning is terminal.

Every newspaper and magazine also has a site, so if the organization is large enough you will be able to research any news items or articles via one of the lovely search engines we mentioned earlier.

But for the real lowdown, you may want to talk to people who are working, or have worked, for the company. The Internet was first developed by academics as a system for sharing information. Or as a failsafe place for the military to communicate in case they blew up the world. (I just put that in to forestall the correspondence from all you conspiracists.) In the spirit of the former you'll find all sorts of advice and opinions in spades. The best places to head for the lowdown on pretty much any subject you can imagine are the Usenet newsgroups. I think I can guarantee that whatever your career choice, and whatever your query, you will find someone on Usenet with the answer. You can seek them out via a search engine, although some recruitment sites also include the facility to swap information with other users.

Before you venture into participating in this wonderful world of cyber-babble, it's a good idea to say nothing for a while – because these people have developed a whole protocol of their own. Some of it applies across the whole Internet, but some of it will be specific to individual groups. So don't just barge in there 'SHOUTING' (using capital letters) your 'FAQ' (frequently asked question) until you've 'lurked' (kept schtum and watched what everyone else is saying).

Or else you may get 'flamed' (a severe telling off. With nasty sweary words sometimes).

Just as in any community, you'll find that there are some nutjobs in there, but you'll quickly be able to differentiate them from the genuinely helpful folk. In the interest of your own safety, though, you should be wary of using your own full, real name. Initials or a nickname will suffice. And never give out your contact details in any public forum on the Internet. Even your e-mail address. Unscrupulous operators, cyber-stalkers, embittered former spouses and those who are plain bonkers are potentially all out there.

Some chat sites also have areas where you virtually 'talk' to other people about careers, but it's probably best to approach most of these with some scepticism. Even if you do manage to suss out the extraordinary code the chatters are using, because of the random nature of the beast you may struggle to find any form of sentient being with anything useful to tell you.

When it comes to browsing specific vacancies, the World Wide Web is your virtual oyster, offering jobs and more jobs beyond your wildest dreams. It's still fair to say that a preponderance of them are oriented towards new technology businesses, but there's more than enough for the rest of us to go at.

Remember that we said all newspapers and magazines are now online (except my local weekly rag. Sometimes I think I live in the town that time forgot)? That means their situations vacant columns are all available to you at any time, for free, and without any

GET LOST Avoid any careers or recruitment site that directly asks you for money. And be wary to the point of scornful of any site that asks for credit card details. Even if they say it's only for identification purposes. The other thing you don't want is your in-box to be overflowing with junk – or 'spam' – so look out for little ticky boxes that you need to click on to stop your address being sold on by the site to a host of other companies.

tedious trips to the newsagents. You'll find that many of the local and regional publications will have 'Jobs' listed in their index, but when you click on that, you'll actually be directed to a recruitment site. Which is what we'll deal with next.

Overleaf is a list of some of the recruitment sites I think are pretty useful. I'm not giving them the Parragon Books Golden Seal Of Approval, I'm just saying that they're worth checking out. As well as acting as a dirty great virtual situations vacant column, there are other services offered by many recruitment sites that make them worth visiting.

Most of them are run by people who have made careers and recruitment their profession. So in the 'ever-changing job market', where better to look for the latest information than a medium that is potentially updated daily? You'll find a plethora of advice about the current thinking on CVs, interview techniques, career planning and job seeking. If you're new to the Internet, you'll quickly discover the 'portal' system, whereby each site is linked or acts as a gateway to more sites that may prove helpful. For free and highly professional careers advice, some of the best sites are those run by universities for their graduates.

Some sites will also offer a more bespoke approach to recruitment, offering to personalize your job hunt. There are two principal ways this can happen. The first is when you fill in an on line form, they then search all incoming vacancies and periodically e-mail you with suitable vacancies. That's definitely worth a shot, though obviously if you find all manner of entirely unsuitable positions dumped into your in-box three times weekly, you should unsubscribe from the service and try another.

Others offer a service whereby they keep your CV on line for all to look at, and as a refinement, some will even match you up with available vacancies and automatically send it to the employer. That one probably needs thinking about more than once. As we shall see in a future section, one of the skills you need to learn is that of adapting your CV for each vacancy. If you have a standard one that goes out to everybody,

GET IN TOUCH

There are countless sites out there of varying degrees of usefulness when it comes to job hunting. You could spend the rest of your life and beyond looking at them all. You should soon get the hang of sussing out which ones are right for you and which ones are out of date or completely useless. Here, in no specific order – and with no cast-iron guarantees – are ten that we believe are of some merit. They're all British based, they all deal with a variety of vacancies and none of them make stuff up.

- www.employmentservice.gov.uk
- www.jobsearch.co.uk
- www.jobs.co.uk
- www.jobsunlimited.co.uk
- www.jobhunter.co.uk
- www.jobsite.co.uk
- www.jobline.co.uk
- www.jobsnetwork.co.uk
- www.jobpilot.co.uk
- www.monster.co.uk

you'll obviously not be able to do that. Now, I don't know about you, but I would prefer to entrust the process of actually applying for a job to me and me alone. And if you're already in employment and don't want your employer to know you are looking for a position elsewhere, then steer well clear of this method. Do I have to spell out the danger for you? Believe me, it has happened.

Do please be careful when entrusting your career to completely anonymous people whom you only know though a fancy pop-up graphic. There are some real idiots out there running websites – and, even worse, some proper crooks. There is practically no official regulation of Internet recruitment sites, which means that you and I could set one up together in your shed with an elastic band and some post-it notes.

If you are thinking about signing up with an online recruiting service, then there are a few things you can do to check them out. Look for any accreditation from an official body. The AGCAS, or Association of Graduate Recruiters, is a likely one. Be suspicious of any site that doesn't carry contact details beyond an e-mail address. No land-based address or telephone number could mean that they don't want you to get in touch with them. Generally speaking, the more personal information they require you to give them, the better. It should mean that they're not just bulk mailing thousands of CVs to hundreds of employers, whether they want them or not. Finally, look closely at the vacancies they list. If you see a load of them that have passed their deadline for applications, then whoever is running the site is a lazy blighter. One even hears of sites that just steal vacancies en masse from their competitors to make them look bigger than they are. And don't quote me on this, but rumour has it that there are sites who just make vacancies up.

More and more often you'll find you have the opportunity to actually apply for jobs online. There'll be a proper form and everything, with bits for you to type in the relevant information and a host of ticky boxes to scroll through. Nothing wrong with that. I quite like the idea. Principally because my heart sinks whenever I have to hand-write any sort of form. From my handwriting, a graphologist would probably have me down as a web-footed Apache with the delirium tremens. However, as with e-mail, you should watch out for that rush of blood. Play it safe. Print the form out. Fill it in longhand. Then fill it in again online. Then print it off again. Read it and check it, preferably some time after you initially filled it in. And only after all of that can you dispatch it into cyberspace. One tiny mistake on a form like that will result in your application visiting the recycle bin faster than you can possibly imagine. It's worth taking time over.

GET TICKED OFF
- Get online today
- Keep all e-mails brief, formal and polite
- Never pay for online recruitment services
- Protect your privacy
- Print off and check all e-mail and online application forms for errors before you send them off

GET SOME
HELP

How are we doing so far? I guess you've decided what it is that you want to do, and found out what training you need. You've started looking around, doing your research and using the Internet on a limited regular basis. Is it all going according to plan? Do you need some help? Someone to talk to? Someone to thrash out the details and put it all in perspective? It can't hurt, can it? Particularly if you've been out of work for a while, or you're drudging away in some job you really can't stand – the whole thing can get a little confusing then. You know that 'rabbit frozen in the headlights' thing that can go on when you're making major changes and decisions? Well, everyone gets it, and when they do they should get some help.

So what help is specifically available to you as an avid job seeker? Officially there's quite a lot. Governments don't like unemployment – it messes with their popularity, and if that dips they could end up having to buy a copy of this book. So in order to keep those figures as low as possible – and perhaps to hedge their bets – they put a lot of resources into making sure there's the maximum amount of advice available.

But before we get into any official sources of help that may be around, take some time also to check out the unofficial help. What we're hoping here is that you have a loving and supportive network of friends and family to bounce off. That can't be underestimated, just as a way to get your thoughts straight if you find yourself getting skewed around a bit.

And if you're cool with the general state of your head but finding the specifics of the job hunt a little confusing, then do that thing where you talk to people who are doing the job you want to do. At the risk of sounding repetitive, that's always going to be the best way to go. If you find the right people they're going to give you the real lowdown on what the career really entails. Besides, it's always best to learn from other people's mistakes, as opposed to your own. And most of all, because if you do that you're keeping up with your programme of networking yourself into a job. Remember, the people who work there are the ones most likely to know if there's a vacancy on the horizon.

For less personal and specific advice – and this might surprise some people – your local Job Centre is actually a pretty damn good place to start. Time was when they were seen as the last resort for deadlegs looking for minimum wage deals to get the dole off their cases. They are, of course, still where you head if you're unemployed and need to claim benefits. And if you find yourself in that unfortunate position, can I point you in the direction of my book *Everything You Need To Know About Job Hunting* (HarperCollins, 2001)? It has a useful chapter carrying advice on dealing with the vagaries of the benefits system.

But even if you aren't looking for financial help, checking out the facilities is pretty vital these days. One of the most significant advancements has been the introduction in the bigger Job Centres of the 'Jobpoint'. Instead of the traditional rows of cards on boards carrying vacancies, what you now get is banks of groovy touch-sensitive computer screens. You need to know that the Employment Service, who run the Job Centres, have a whole bunch of staff that you never see who spend their time inputting all the latest vacancies into one great database. So the Jobpoints are being updated on a permanent basis. The screens are easy to use and you can search under pretty much any criteria. First off you specify what sort of work you're looking for – and the range is about as wide as you can imagine. Yes the £3.80 an hour burger flippers are there, but so are the lawyers, accountants and computer programmers.

When I was testing the system out I even found jobs I could do! Seriously. They actually have a section for writers. You can look in the area where you live, or pan out to include the whole country and even some jobs abroad. You can specify full-time, part-time, temporary or permanent work.

When you've narrowed it down to where you get full details – description, salary, hours and location – for a job or jobs that you fancy, you hit the print icon and it churns out a little slip, which you take to a member of staff. They'll discuss the position with you and make contact with the employer on your behalf to arrange an interview, or get an application form sent out to you.

I know it sounds a bit geeky to use the word 'exciting', but for me this is one of the best and most effective innovations in the field of job seeking that I

GET IN TOUCH The Employment Service database is also available online by hitting www.employmentservice.gov.uk and by telephone on 0845 6060 234 (charged at local rates). They reckon they have access to over 300,000 nationwide vacancies on any given day, and the given days are Monday to Friday, 9 a.m. to 6 p.m., and Saturday from 9 a.m. to 1 p.m. Aside from arranging interviews and sending out application forms, they have a three-way calling facility that allows you to speak directly to the employer during the call. This option is particularly useful if you live some place where there is no Job Centre.

know of. Obviously it doesn't replace the 'hidden vacancy' method – after all, you're still competing with a bunch of other people for every position. But the speed and regularity with which the system is updated really means that a daily visit to the Job Centre wouldn't be excessive.

Aside from the cool and groovy Jobpoints (respect to the designers for their grasp of ergonomics), the Job Centre is now pretty much the focal point for all work-related stuff. You'll be able to get advice and information on special initiatives in employment and training in your region. You'll see notification of Company Open Days, Jobfairs and training days.

They'll also point you in the direction of your local Careers Office. For although the Job Centre is a great place to look for vacancies, to attempt to claim the pittance that is a 'Job seeker's allowance' and to get general advice, there is a more sophisticated level of help available.

Somewhere near you, and God alone knows where, will be a Careers Counselling Service. Possibly several.

Actually, that's why you're best off asking at the Job Centre, because it's pointless asking God. For some strange reason, pretty much every single Careers Office in the country goes under a different name. The one in Warrington is called 'Connexions', which sounds more like a massage parlour than a good source for advice. And in Wales they're called Gyrfau A Mwy. Which could mean anything. Whatever they're called, they're contracted by the Department for Education and Employment to offer advice on working and training.

The issue can be slightly confused by the fact that there may well be different offices for different groups of people. A lot of the higher profile ones you'll find are for those who are aged 18–24; in fact, if you're between these ages, they've probably found you already. Part of the programme is to send careers advisors into schools and colleges to ensure that everyone has access to the service before they head off into the world of work.

Once you've identified where the Careers Counselling Service is that caters for you, then you really should get yourself along and make an appointment. The range of services tends to vary somewhat, but the very least you can expect is the listening ear and helpful mouth of a careers professional who knows his or her onions when it comes to the specifics of landing the job you want.

Some places also have free access to computers, photocopiers and telephones specifically for the job seeker. They are likely to be of the most help if you are actually unemployed at present, but don't by any means let that deter you from enquiring if you are seeking to change your career.

The next place you may want to stop off in your quest for help is an 'employment agency'. I put that term in quotation marks because there's room for confusion here on what exactly it is that constitutes an 'employment agency'. It won't have escaped your notice that there's a whole bunch of firms out there with nice premises and big fancy ads offering to find you all kinds of work.

What you need to be aware of – and totally clear

about when you sign on – is whether the one you picked is an employment 'business' or a traditional 'agency'. Both types of organization have to be licensed by the Department of Trade and Industry, who set down rules on how they should operate. You need to be familiar with the rules and to be able to differentiate, because it will make a difference to your money and possibly your relationship with a potential employer.

An agency is basically engaged by an employer to find their staff. Sometimes the employer pays the agency a fee to recruit all their workers; more likely they'll pay a percentage of the employee's first year's salary. The agency puts notices in their window, takes out advertisements and trawls their database for the ideal candidate. They make the suggestions to the employer and send people along for interviews. Once the appointment has been made, the employee has nothing more to do with the agency. They work for the employer and any financial arrangement that an agency makes with your boss is, strictly speaking, none of your business.

Although often referred to as an 'agency', an employment business is a whole other entity. If you sign up with one, they find you the work. They sort out your contract, they deal with your tax and National Insurance. The company you are working for pays the employment business, which usually takes a cut and passes the money on to you. Confusion can arise because a lot of agencies also run employment businesses at the same time. That means that they can put the word 'agency' on their sign outside, but they might be getting you work under the auspices of their employment business division. You need to be absolutely clear about which method of working – and more importantly, which method of getting paid – you're signing up for.

Employment businesses are most common in the fields of temporary and casual work. Obviously it makes sense when you consider that under those circumstances you may only actually be working at one place for a matter of weeks, or even days. However, in some respects you fall into a bit of a no man's land when you take work via a business. Quite a few of them do not contract you as an 'employee'. As we've seen, you're also not an 'employee' of the place you're working at. This means that you don't get some of the employment rights that you might normally expect. These, for example:

• Redundancy pay
• Proper pay-slips
• Notice to quit
• Sick pay
• Appeals against unfair dismissal

So that's another thing you need to check out carefully. If the employment business is classing you as an employee, then they are responsible for ensuring you've got those rights. If they aren't (and the majority don't for that very reason), then you could at some point run into trouble if things don't work out.

There have been cases where temporary or casual workers have taken employment businesses to industrial tribunal over such matters, and won on the

GET LOST Unless you're a nanny, a model, an artist or a writer, an employment agency or employment business can't charge you any fee whatsoever for finding you work. So don't part with cash. Some of them will find ways of extracting money from you. They might encourage you to pay for career counselling sessions – like the ones that are free at your nearest government-accredited office. They could offer to charge you for doing your CV – which we'll be showing you how to do for free in a later chapter. Or they may have a series of selection tests on offer, for a fee, which will guide you towards the right career. For what they're worth, you can find them for nothing in library books and on the Internet. The law states that if they do take money off you they have to state clearly what it's for. If you feel you've been ripped off, then grass them up to the DTI. Their hotline is 08459 555105.

basis that the business had set a precedent in establishing a relationship whereby they acted as an employer. They hired and fired, paid weekly wages, administered tax and insurance etc. But that's obviously a lengthy process to go through, with no guarantee of success. So it's best to get straight beforehand exactly what your situation is.

Here's a rundown of some of the rules that the Department of Trade and Industry lays down for employment businesses and agencies:

- Neither an employment business or agency can charge you any kind of fee for seeking or finding you work.
- Employment agencies aren't allowed to offer you any kind of financial incentive for using their services.
- Employment agencies that propose to charge a worker a fee for services other than job finding must, before providing services, give the worker a clearly legible written statement detailing the service and the proposed charge.
- Employment agencies must not make the provision

of job-finding services contingent upon the worker using any of their other services.

- If an employment agency receives money on your behalf they must give it to you within ten days of receipt or, if for some peculiar reason you've asked them to hang on to it for you, they must pay it into a special client account.

- An employment business must give you full details in writing of the terms and conditions of employment, including whether you're under contract or are self-employed, the kind of work you may be supplied to do and the minimum rates of pay for such work; any subsequent changes must also be given to you in writing.

- An employment business must give you all available information about the nature of the hirer's business, the kind of work and the hours and rate of pay applicable and make appropriate enquiries to find out whether you have any qualification which is required by law for the work and that performance of the work (whether in the United Kingdom or abroad) will not contravene the law.

- An employment business must not prohibit or restrict you in any way from entering the direct employment of a hirer and must not refuse to pay you because they have not been paid by the hirer.

It's good, that last one. So bear it in mind. It's not unheard of for an employment business to refuse to give people work because they came to a private arrangement with one of their clients. Note too that they have to pay you when they say they will. Even if they haven't been paid by the employer yet.

When it comes to choosing which 'agency' is right for you, there's obviously no substitute for a personal recommendation. If you can find someone who has dealt with a particular agency before, you'll be able to get the inside dope.

The other good thing to do is actually visit the premises if you can. That way you can not only check out how they deal with you, but also how they're doing for other people. A brief chat in reception or outside the gaff with their other clients could tell you all you

GET REAL

Phoebe was pretty well qualified, hard working and personable. She'd been out of the job market for some time because she'd raised a bunch of kids. They'd got older and so she started looking around for work. She was busy doing all the stuff you're supposed to do in order to get work and decided that to tide her over she'd join a local temping agency. They got her some work. So that was cool. But she noticed that the agency office was permanently in a state of chaos, she had to wait ages to see anyone and sometimes they cocked up the details of the jobs she went to. She took the initiative and the next time she saw one of the partners she offered to come in a day a week and do some administration. He agreed and within three months she was managing that office on a full-time basis.

need to know. We're not including a highly recommended list here because even though an organization might be basically okay to deal with, how efficient and helpful they are to you mainly depends on your local branch and the staff there.

So you're going to have to stay frosty and do the digging yourself. Just watch out for the ones that are trying to push you into a field or career that you don't want or are not suitable for, just because they need to earn their fee and an employer has been on the phone six times an hour demanding to see people. And don't buy any hogwash about how you have to be 'exclusive' to them. You don't. Keep your options open. And watch out for that other hogwash about how you should refer any leads or offers back to them, even if you sourced them yourself. That's the easiest money they make. You spend all that time and effort administering and researching your job search and they step in at the last minute to charge the employer a whacking great fee.

If you're a highly qualified specialist in some field or

other – catering, teaching, law, medical, lorry driving etc. – then you should be able to find an agency or business that deals directly with your profession without too much trouble. And you'd be well advised to do so.

A good employment agency or business will have access to vacancies that aren't always on general release. They'll have established good relationships with employers, and will be highly specific about what their clients are looking for. They should be able to sit down with you and give you the full lowdown on the organizations they work for, including what they do, their reputation, skills required, future prospects and how their selection process works. If they arrange an interview for you, they should also give you a thorough briefing on what to expect, perhaps even some background on who is likely to be doing the interview and the best way to deal with them. As a third party they may also give you a better 'feedback' service than the actual employer.

If you do find a highly motivated and scrupulous

agency who are able to find you well-paid work – and they are out there – then treat them with respect. Turn up at the workplace and do the things you're asked to do, and you'll find that that very fact will put you at the top of their list whenever they have anything else on their books.

GET TICKED OFF

- If you're feeling bewildered, talk to friends and family, just to get your head straight
- Use your local Job Centre – daily isn't too often
- Find out where your nearest Careers Office is and plunder their resources
- Check out the credentials of an employment agency or business really carefully before you sign up
- Never part with any money to an employment agency or business

GET THAT CV **S** ORTED

Ooohhh. Scary CV time. All that trauma, sweat, blood and tears over a couple of sides of A4. The way some people go on, you would think that it was the single most important document you will ever possess.

GET LOST Everywhere you go – on- and off-line – there are people prepared to take hard cash off you in return for writing your CV. Don't let them have it. Using models from books like this one, you will quickly pick up an idea as to how it should look. The actual writing of the thing can be accomplished with only a couple of hours' training on a computer. And if you're worried at all about your spelling, grammar or layout skills, then there are a host of experts specifically employed by the government to ensure that you get it right. They can and will advise you at your local Careers Office. For nowt. You also get to keep the disk, which means that you can amend it any time you need to. For nowt.

Some charlatans even write whole books about how to do one. Pages and pages of complex stuff on how to write two pages of dead simple stuff.

Of course you have to have one, and of course it has to look good, and it can be a really useful tool in your job search. But in comparison to a really good letter, an articulate phone call or an impressive interview, it's not really that big a deal.

To put it into context, research has been done which suggests that on average a CV is read for between twenty and thirty seconds. My own informal research (just asking people responsible for reading CVs) suggests that time scale may be erring on the generous side. Which perhaps leads us to two conclusions. First, that you shouldn't generate too much angst about the thing, and second, that you should keep it as brief but effective as possible. Here's the key phrase for this entire chapter:

IF IN DOUBT LEAVE IT OUT

Just to get the technical stuff out of the way, CV stands for curriculum vitae, which is Latin for 'course of life'. Sometimes known as a 'résumé', specifically by our friends in the States, it's a list of what you've done with particular emphasis on how that qualifies you to do a job.

The only real hard-and-fast rule about yours is that it should look good. Which means it should be well laid out, easy to read and it shouldn't be too long. So you have to do it on a computer. Old-fashioned longhand, or even a typewriter, just won't do. If you're not going to make an investment in a computer at home you should at least splash out on a disk so that you can take a permanent record from whichever computer you work on.

There are three good reasons for this, as follows:

- It's easier to lay out properly
- You can update it any time
- It shows an employer that you have mastered basic word-processing skills

You need to be able to update it periodically, not just because stuff might happen – you gain new qualifications or relevant experience – but because you'll probably want to tailor it a little for each new job you apply for. Say, for example, you've still got your heart set on vicaring, but a paucity of funds means that you've been forced to apply for a job at Impregnation Services Ltd. It's unlikely that they're going to be in any way impressed by the standard CVs you've been sending out to bishops, which punch up your marrying and burying skills. So you're going to have to find a way of emphasizing very quickly the skills and training you have that make you suitable for work in light engineering.

The content and the layout are very much interrelated, so perhaps the best thing to do is show you an example of a CV, and then go through it step by step. The one below is by no means definitive, so don't just go copying it. It's only here to start you off.

Havelock Dayne
Curriculum Vitae

Havelock Dayne
77 Righteous Street
Godalming
Surrey B4 G0D

Tel: 23820 1 4211212
Mobile: 6213109147 215151
E-mail: havelock@elvis.com
Dob: 25.12.1970

- Fully trained vicar
- Experienced jumble sale organizer
- National Vicar Society –
  Best Wedding Service Award 1999
- Comprehensive hymn book
  collection

Education

1981–86: St Simon's Comprehensive School: GCSEs in Religious Education, English, Maths, Metalwork, Art.

1986–88: Godalming Sixth Form College: A Levels in Religious Education, English, Metalwork.

1990–93: Canterbury University: First Class Honours degree in Theology.

1995–96: Diploma in Advanced Vicaring (night class).

2000–Present: Open University course in Effective Sermonizing.

Additional Courses

First Aid

Computer Skills

Advanced Jumble Sale Coordination

Employment

Current: Assistant impregnator at Impregnation Services Ltd. Volunteer Warden at St Lona's Church, Godalming. Duties include organizing flower rota, supervising choir boys and emptying poor box.

1994–99: Full-time Vicar at St Fay's in Lower Godalming. Average congregation of 300. Twenty-five sinners converted per year. Presided over 121 weddings, 693 christenings and 390 funerals.

1990–93: Sales Assistant at 'God Is Dead Good' Christian Bookshop, Canterbury. Duties included dealing with customers, handling sales and stock control.

1986–88: General Assistant at Ivalot & Sons Impregnators of Godalming.

So what do we have here? Well, we have a nicely laid out document which is about a page and a bit at A4 size, it should be printed in black on white paper, and it should be entirely gimmick free. So no funny pictures, smiley icons or attempts at humour – they could rebound on you if the reader doesn't share your love of Pokemon or old *Terry & June* gags.

We also have some specifics worth looking at. From the top, then. You'll see that Havelock has included all his contact details. Which is the right thing to do. The only possible exception would be if you were working some place and you didn't want your current employer to know you were looking for a job elsewhere – then you wouldn't include your daytime phone number. Otherwise, include the lot. All phone numbers, faxes and addresses.

He's also included his date of birth. Now this isn't mandatory and there are sometimes good arguments for omitting it. This is the first bit of the CV anyone's going to look at, so if you feel that your extreme youth or extreme age is likely to prejudice an employer, then feel free to leave it out. Just be aware that a smart personnel or human resources manager will work it out pretty pronto from the rest of the information. Obviously it's entirely wrong for an employer to make a judgement based on a person's age. But in a real world it does happen. Remember that the CV is there to support the rest of your application for the job, so it shouldn't carry anything at all that might jeopardize your chances.

IF IN DOUBT LEAVE IT OUT

Perhaps Havelock knows that the bishop to whom he is sending his application will be impressed by the fact that he is only 32 and has already been in charge of a large church. On the other hand, he could be wrong. The bishop might be the kind of man who leans towards the theory that a vicar should have extensive life experience before he can be entrusted with the spiritual welfare and tombola prizes of his flock.

Next up, Havelock has put a bit that is usually referred to and headlined as 'skills and strengths'. More often than not these sections are put at the end of a CV. I don't know why anyone would put the most important things in the place where they are least likely to be looked at, but they do. Sometimes people write this bit as a paragraph: 'I have been a fully trained vicar since 1995 and am an exceptionally good jumble sale organizer. In 1999 my achievements were recognized when I won a national award as . . .' I'm sorry, but I'm getting bored writing it. Even if it isn't always the case, work on the assumption that the best your CV is going to get is a skim read. So get those strong points to stand out somehow.

You've probably noticed that Havelock really has two separate career paths going on. Although the vicaring looms large in this CV, he is currently working at Impregnation Services in some sort of engineering capacity. What he's done is adapt the CV for this particular application so that it emphasizes the former. If he was applying for a job in another engineering company, then he would be sensible to put an entirely different slant on the 'skills and strengths'. Similarly, with his subsequent Education and Employment History, he has dealt very briefly with his current duties and achievements in order to stress what he accomplished as a vicar.

You can also exercise your best judgement when it comes to the Education and Employment sections. Conventionally, Education comes first in chronological order and then Employment in reverse order. Just as they are in the sample above. But you may decide to get the thing that makes you most suited for the job in there as early as possible. If Havelock had switched the order of his education so that it read in reverse, the very first things you'd read would be to do with his impressive training to be a vicar.

Conversely, if he were going for the engineering job, he might want to put his Employment History first and in chronological order. That way his position at

GET IN TOUCH You might disagree with some of the stuff I've written here about CVs. And there are different opinions from mine, so you'd be forgiven for your scepticism. If you want an alternative viewpoint, the Internet is chock full of advice and samples. A good way to collate them all is to go to www.ask.co.uk and type in 'how do I write a CV?'. You'll get an abundance of sites to look at.

Impregnation Services – with a more comprehensive listing of his duties – would be the first thing that struck the reader.

Imagine that whoever is reading your CV is looking for the bit that makes you suitable for the job. They're a busy person and they have a heap of others to get through. Make it easy for them. That way they'll hopefully look at you in a more favourable light into the bargain.

At the end of a CV people often put the names and contact details for their references. Havelock hasn't. He's just got a note to say that they are available. Use your discretion here. Aside from anything else, there is a protection of privacy issue. If you're being diligent in your job search, then it's likely that your CV is going to be seen by a lot of people. It's not going to do you any good to have your poor referee hounded to death by all and sundry. Perhaps much better to wait until you're contacted by a prospective employer before supplying the details. That way you can also brace whoever you've decided to vouch for you, so that they're prepared for the letter or phone call. It's basic good manners, and sensible thinking to ask permission of your referees anyway.

However, if you're applying for a specific job and you have a specific reference that you know is perfect for the application, then do the asking beforehand, and bung them down. Maybe even earlier in the document. If Havelock knows he can get a glowing testimony from the Archbishop of Canterbury, then he'd be daft not to have the guy's name and address under his own details when applying for church gigs. Provided, of course, he'd cleared it with the old AB of C first.

IF IN DOUBT LEAVE IT OUT

Loads of people have a section at the end of their CV that they headline as 'Hobbies' or 'Interests'. Havelock hasn't. It's not so much that he has no hobbies and interests as the fact that he doesn't feel they are relevant to the position. Only you can make that decision with regards to the job that you're after. If you're a school leaver looking for your first job, your CV isn't going to be very long. So there is an argument for including your other interests to give the employer an idea of what kind of person you are, and what engages your enthusiasm. I don't want to come across all didactic here, but if you do decide to list them, and the list reads:

- Watching TV
- Listening to music
- Playing computer games
- Going out

then you should definitely leave that lot out. It doesn't make you stand out from any other applicant and the reader might be forgiven for thinking that all you do with your life is sit around waiting for the pub to open.

IF IN DOUBT LEAVE IT OUT

Just a few words of reassurance for those of you who are leaving education and embarking on your job search for the first time. Don't worry about the fact that your CV may appear to be a little on the short side. The employers will be fully aware of what's going on with you, and

GET REAL

Daytime Emma (so called to differentiate her from another Emma who worked in the same bar at night, and because it suited her sunnier disposition) had never really had what you'd call a 'proper' job. She'd temped and freelanced and worked part-time, but nothing with any definite career path.

Emma had always fancied travelling, though, and became aware of a large number of vacancies at the local airport. She felt that maybe it could be a way in to finding something that took her abroad. Emma applied for a position as an immigration clerk and to get around the problem of her somewhat disparate CV, she submitted a document that carried the bare minimum contact details and one A4 page with signed quotes from the people she had been working for. All of which emphasized her aforementioned sunny disposition, her flexibility and consummate people skills. Last I heard, she was in Singapore.

won't expect you to have tons of experience. What they will be looking for is attitude, initiative and a willingness to work. You could even put stuff like that in your CV. One guy I know put down a couple of the more positive comments from his last school report.

And while I'm reassuring folk, here's some advice for the person who's been out of the job game for a while. Don't get het up about the 'gaps' that some recruitment 'experts' might suck their teeth and shake their heads at. I bet there's a damned good reason why you weren't in full-time employment, and whatever it was it doesn't prevent from you being an exemplary employee now. If you look closely at Havelock's CV you'll notice that there's nothing going on with him for the whole of 1989. I bet most of you didn't even notice that. The most likely explanation is that he bummed around a bit between sixth form college and university, perhaps unclear of exactly what it was that he wanted to do. The best way for him to deal with that hiatus is to have an answer prepared in the event of it coming up at the interview.

In these days of increased freelance and temporary contract jobs, many of us would find it difficult to produce a traditional, sequential work history for our CVs. We perhaps jump from job to job, maybe doing a number of things at one time, some of them not directly related. All of which means we need to give even more thought to tailoring the document for the specific employer we're approaching. Again, it shouldn't really be a cause for concern. An enlightened employer will recognize where you're at, and hopefully appreciate that it is likely to make you more flexible and creative in your work.

One of the most important parts of this whole CV business is the letter that should always accompany it. Obviously it should complement the CV in so far as it should be well presented and grammatically correct, with no spelling mistakes. But you should also assume that the letter is more likely to get read than the CV. And in some cases they'll read the former and file the latter.

You don't want to annoy people by making the

covering letter as long as the CV, but you can take the opportunity to at least reiterate your strong points in a succinct fashion. Like this, perhaps:

Havelock Dayne
77 Righteous Street
Godalming
Surrey B4 G0D

Mobile: 6213109147 215151
E-mail: havelock@elvis.com

Bishop B. Inchpenny
The Bishopry
12 Tribes Street
Godalming
Surrey B4 JC2

2.3.02

Dear Bishop Inchpenny,

I am very interested in the position of vicar at St Stanley's and would appreciate you considering me for the post.

I have enclosed my CV, which I believe shows I have the right qualifications and training for the position, including the following:

• Fully trained Vicar
• Experienced Jumble Sale Organizer
• National Vicar Society Best Wedding Service Award 1999
• Comprehensive Hymn Book Collection

Perhaps I could contact you next week to make an appointment to have a chat about the post.

Yours sincerely,
Havelock Dayne

As a man of the cloth, the bishop, and any other employer looking for good staff, will appreciate the concept of 'not hiding your light under a bushel'. In other words, don't ever be shy of making a point about how good you would be at the job on offer. But for heaven's sake, don't tell any lies. Obviously, this would be a particularly bad move in Havelock's case, given the nature of the job. But it's a rule that should hold true for all of us. Employers are becoming increasingly scrupulous in checking claims about education, qualifications and experience, and if you lie about any of them, you'll not get the job for two reasons. One, you're not qualified to do it, and secondly, no one really wants to employ a liar. You should also resist the temptation to exaggerate or inflate the truth to the point at which you can be caught out. A classic case is where a candidate with a very basic command of a language describes themselves as 'fluent'. It happened to someone I knew who had a beginner's knowledge of Spanish. One of the interviewing panel was Spanish, and she was conducting the interview in her native tongue . . .

IF IN DOUBT LEAVE IT OUT

You should perhaps look at your CV as an organic thing. Clearly, it will change as you develop more skills and experience, but it will also improve as a document if you take time to refine it. It's inadvisable to just bang out the same old copy to every employer. Treat each instance as unique. Read the job description and respond accordingly. Think through what you know you have that the employer wants and make a feature of it. And if you've been job seeking for a while without success, then give the CV a bit of an overhaul to see if that helps.

GET TICKED OFF

- Never pay for the professional production of a CV. There's tons of free help available
- Keep your CV concise. If it's more than two pages it's probably too long
- Always use a computer to produce your CV. It looks good
- Reiterate the main points of your CV in your covering letter
- Keep your CV constantly updated

GET THAT
APPLICATION
IN

Although we sincerely believe that the best way to get yourself a job is to seek out the 'hidden vacancy', it would be foolish to ignore the most traditional route to employment. The one where you pick up a newspaper, trawl through the situations vacant section, spot something that suits you and get your application in.

Obviously, the first step here is to get hold of the relevant publications – and to give yourself the edge, get them before anyone else does. In a lot of cases the Internet is a good place to start: while some national newspapers will publish their job sections once a week, their online recruitment advertisements are updated daily. The same applies for a lot of professional and trade periodicals.

For those rags that don't put their jobs online then you need to be first out of the blocks when it comes to reading the ads, and the library is one of the best places to be for many of them. Not only will it save you a small fortune, but you'll also get first shot at those publications that send out subscription copies before they hit the shops.

For local daily and weekly newspapers, the best way to get out of the traps first is to find out when copies arrive at the local office from the printers, and make sure you pick up your copy directly from there. For national papers you're just going to have to get up dead, dead early. Or stay up dead, dead late. In some cities early editions of national papers are out on the streets before midnight the preceding day.

So there they are, all those boxes of varying size, crammed with jargon. Golden opportunities and demanding criteria. And somewhere in there, you are hoping to find the job you dreamed of. Now, maybe you've got a superbrain that can assimilate all that information, sift through it and have the relevant jobs applied for before breakfast. I don't have one of those brains. I'll just stand over here with the stupid people. If I'm scouring the *Guardian* on a Monday for potential writing jobs, I have to do it twice. One general skim through to see if anything leaps out at me, and then one slow look at each ad on each page. On particularly stupid days I take a pencil or my finger and rest it on each individual advertisement until I've read through it and made entirely sure that I'm too stupid to apply for it.

I mark with a cross in the margin any positions that I might consider applying for, and after I've been through the paper twice I cut out the ones that I'm sure I could do (checking the back of each one before I cut it out. Yes, I have been that stupid). As I have also learned, the hard way, about the tendency of things cut out of newspapers to go missing, I staple them immediately into my diary. It's a very good idea to keep job advertisements on file. Of course, they carry all the details of the job you're applying for, and you may need to refer to them at some point during your application. But they'll also give you contact details and information on the company in the event that you want to make a speculative approach at some point in the future.

Sometimes you might see an advertisement for a position that you really fancy, but the specification for the job looks way out of your league. Keep the advertisement anyway and keep an eye on the press.

If it appears again in a few weeks it means that they've had trouble filling the position, perhaps because their expectations were just too damned high. You could write a covering letter that includes a couple of sentences along the lines of:

'While I have many of the skills and much of the experience required in your advertisement, I am not yet fully conversant with all of the procedures listed. However, I have proved myself very quick to learn additional skills, and so wondered if you would consider my application.'

It's probably not a good idea to send such a letter very often. Certainly not to support applications where you patently have no experience or training for the position. Take a kind of seventy/thirty position on it. If you've got about seven out of ten of the attributes they're looking for, then it's maybe worth a shot.

You also need to figure out exactly why the organization has opted to take out an advertisement in a newspaper. It's an expensive process and can be time consuming if sacks full of applications start pouring in. Employers really do prefer not to have to go to all that trouble and expense. They're still hoping that the perfect candidate is just going to fall magically out of the sky. After you've figured out why they took the advertisement, you may need to tailor your application accordingly. These are the three main reasons an organization has for advertising a job in a paper:

- They have lots of vacancies to fill
- They are obliged by law or policy to advertise
- They just can't find anyone any other way

The first instance is the most likely. Maybe a new supermarket or factory is opening in the area, and they need a large number of staff in a hurry. Maybe it's seasonal work. This factory near me makes cakes, for example. And the mother of Mark Owen, ex of Take That, works there, apparently. Around October they always take space in the local paper advertising for people to stand on their production lines in the run-up to Christmas. If you figure out that you're dealing with a large hirer in a hurry, then speed is of the essence. Usually that kind of employer is not looking for highly skilled or qualified people and to a large extent it's going to be a case of first come, first served. Remember that everyone who works there is likely to know someone who is looking for a job, and they're going to get first bite of the cherry. One would imagine that Mark Owen has been tipped off by his old mum, and has got his application in even as I write.

The fastest way to get in first is to call round. If the advertisement says you need an application form, then go right round there and ask for one. Otherwise you'll write or ring and the thing won't turn up for a couple of days. Take your CV with you, and it may be that you can fill out an application and hand it in on the spot. Maybe you'll even get to see someone. If the company is large enough they will have appointed someone specifically to deal with applications; until they come flooding in, that person may be twiddling their thumbs and having to resort to making paperclip sculptures.

If the advertisement says you can apply by letter, then get the letter written pronto, and again drop it in by hand. If it's impractical for you to get round there, then see if you can't get your application in by fax or e-mail, as they're the second fastest methods.

Of course, you may do all that rushing around, and for all you know the personnel department has a policy of putting all applications in a big pile with a view to wading through them all at once in a couple of weeks. Which is tough, but you can't really make that assumption, so don't.

Some job hunters hedge their bets by sending in more than one application form in more than one format. Perhaps they drop one in, post one and then e-mail just to be on the safe side. It's not a bad idea if you're dealing with a large employer. It may be that more then one person looks at applications, and what gets rejected by one gets shortlisted by another.

It's definitely not a good idea in the second instance, where an organization is obliged by law or policy to advertise. You're usually looking at an official post, perhaps in government or education, which will be administered by a professional personnel or human resources department.

You're probably also looking at a lengthier and more thorough selection procedure, and almost certainly a much more demanding application form. So ensure that you get hold of that as soon as possible, check the closing date, and get it in on time, leaving yourself enough time to fill it out in accordance with the advice below.

The comment I'm about to make may seem blindingly obvious, but every other job-seeking book points it out, so I will too. Never send an application in after the closing date. I'll add this codicil, though. If you do see a job advertised that you know you can do, and you've missed the application deadline, there's nothing to stop you ringing them up on the off chance and explaining the situation. Perhaps they're behind with their processing, or haven't found the ideal candidate yet. Even if you get knocked back on that particular job, it could be that you make a useful contact for anything else that may come up.

At this point, I'd like to make an outrageous allegation. You know those jobs that are advertised because the law or policy states they must be? Well, loads of them are already taken long before the advertisement appears. They've been promised to someone who has already worked there for five years, someone who could do the job standing on their head and always stands their round in the bar after work. You know it's true.

You do not, of course, have any way of knowing if that's the case or not; you might suspect something if you get to interview stage and discover that the person who gets the job is the only one who travelled to the interview by lift. But don't be deterred. Even if you reckon that's what's going on, go for the job with as much enthusiasm and dedication as you do normally. There must be a vacancy elsewhere if they've moved the current prime candidate into this one. Also, if you really are in an environment where who you know matters as much as what you know, then you need to get to know some people if you want to work there. An interview, albeit spurious, is a good way to get your foot in the door.

Interestingly, when an organization is driven by 'policy' in its recruitment process, part of that policy includes an obligation to give 'feedback' to unsuccessful candidates. Always check out whether this is available and, if so, take advantage of it. Sometimes the feedback is provided verbally, so it gives you another chance to establish a relationship with a recruiter. Be positive and proactive during this process. Listen carefully to what the recruiter has to say, and pick up on anything that may give you a chance to say something along the lines of, 'So if I get that qualification/acquire those skills, you would consider me for a position in the future?'

If an advertisement is in a paper because the company just can't find anyone in any other way, then you have to ask yourself why. With some practice you can learn to read between the lines of job advertisement copy and suss out those that are simply rubbish jobs

GET IN TOUCH For all the lowdown on the latest methods used by conmen to part you from your cash, take a look at www.crimes-of-persuasion.com. Although it's an American site, many of the cons exposed are in use here in the UK, or soon will be. There are specific sections on employment-related scams, and a useful forum whereby you can learn from the bitter experiences of those who've already been taken for a ride.

that no sane person would want – or those that are scams no sensible person would fall for. Anything, for example, that offers a 'millionaire lifestyle' means exactly that. But not for you. For the person who took the ad. It's fair to say that anyone who asks you to part with money before you start work is out to con you.

Whatever means you use to source a job – whether via adverts, personal contacts or an agency – at some point you're going to find yourself looking at an application form. It has to be said that they're usually pretty horrible. I've seen loads of them and if I've ever been tempted to apply for a 'straight' job, there's been many a time I've taken one long look at one long form and decided that I'll stick with what I've got.

They also present a problem to those of us who have handwriting like an overworked doctor who's been raiding the amphetamine cupboard. It is possible to

GET LOST The most common form of scam secreted amongst the small ads is the Pyramid Selling or Multi-Level Marketing scheme. While it is illegal to engage in such a venture, the shysters who perpetrate them are constantly redefining the nature and title of their businesses in order to get round the law. Even more invidious are those schemes that are presented to you by people you know, perhaps even family or friends. Any time you're approached by anyone with a fabulous scheme to make you wealthy that involves you laying out capital and then 'recruiting' others to do the same, run a mile.

fiddle about with the settings on your computer so that it will print within the parameters of the form. But it's a laborious and potentially soul-destroying activity (in my case, it's more likely to be computer destroying). Besides which, it seems that most employers specify that you should fill out their forms in longhand. Presumably to see whether you can write legibly, although it's not unheard of for more incorporeally inclined corporations to pass samples on to a graphologist.

It goes without saying that when I am prime minister I will introduce legislation that prevents the scrawlers amongst us from being so viciously discriminated against, but until that glorious day I'm afraid we'll just have to take it on the chin. The only possible words of help I can give you are to suggest that you use block capitals and take your time.

In fact, taking your time is good general advice even if you have perfect handwriting. First off, take your time in re-reading the advertisement. The one you cut out and kept filed away some place safe, remember? The majority of application forms arrive accompanied by additional information. There may be documents detailing the organization's policies on health and safety and equal opportunities. Don't necessarily disregard these as superfluous. When my friend Sheehey applied for a job with the local council he clocked the extensive accompanying tome on their equal opportunities policy. He had a hunch that if there was any positive discrimination going on he didn't stand much chance as an able-bodied, white, heterosexual male. So when the issue of his 'attitudes' was raised at the interview, he said, 'I think as a second-generation Irish person living in north Manchester I have encountered enough discrimination myself to ensure that I would never discriminate against anyone else for any reason.' And he got the job.

Crucially, however, there will be notes to read that may be entitled 'Job' or 'Person' specification. These should be read most assiduously of all. For therein lie all the clues as to what exactly this employer is looking for.

Often this specification is divided into two lists, perhaps 'Essential' and 'Desirable' qualities. You need to have a jolly good read and a bit of soul searching before putting pen to paper. Chiefly to ascertain whether or not you genuinely fulfil enough of the criteria to make it worth your while proceeding any further. Any jargon used in the specification document will also give you a good idea of the 'culture' in operation. If you find yourself looking at words or phrases that make no sense to you whatsoever, then you need a crash course in the 'buzzwords' specific to that profession or organization.

If you are pretty convinced that you could do this job, but are struggling with minor details such as jargon, then it can't really hurt to give them a call. A lot of recruiters positively encourage it. Try not to make a negative out of your query and you may even contribute towards creating a good impression that will stand you in good stead further down the line.

So this, for example, would be entirely wrong:

'I'm very sorry to bother you, but I got an application form for the job of vicar at St Uniatz and I just wondered what the hell it means when it

goes on about "Holistic approaches to needs-based pastoral issues?" I mean, call me stupid if you like, but that's just gobbledegook to me.'

Whereas this might be better:

'I'm applying for the position of vicar at St Uniatz and I feel confident that I have pretty much all the attributes required. I was just wondering, however, if I have the same interpretation as you do of "Holistic approaches to needs-based pastoral issues"?'

With any luck, the latter approach should result in not only a clearer understanding but a healthy discussion in which you take the opportunity to demonstrate just how keen and qualified you are.

Once you've assimilated and understood the person specification, you need to start figuring out how exactly you're going to demonstrate that you are the person specified when it comes to filling out the form. But before you do that, provided you've done all the reading – including the form itself – then it is definitely recommended that you take a photocopy of the form. Primarily so that you can have a practice run at filling it in, and also so that you can keep a copy for your files. There may be some time between you sending the form off and getting an interview. You may also be sending out loads of application forms. The chances are that you will forget some of the salient points if you don't have it to refer to.

So, one form for real and one to practise on. And then you just have to get on with it. But here are some of the most common foul-ups when it comes to filling out application forms:

- Writing in the boxes marked 'For Official Use Only'.
- Putting 'Refer to enclosed CV' instead of filling out the requisite boxes.
- Enclosing a CV when specifically requested not to.
- Lying. And most stuff can and will be checked out, you know.
- Stapling additional sheets in. Use a paperclip.
- Crossings out and Tipp-Ex all over the place.
- Over-use of technical terms and jargon. It's worth

remembering that sometimes the person dealing with your application knows little of the terms involved. They are just acting as a personnel filter.

Some of these points might seem petty or obvious, but in real life they comprise the factors most likely to send your application winging its way to the waste paper basket. Work on the premise that whoever is dealing with your application has a huge heap to get through and any forms that cause them distress will end up scrumpled underneath the remains of their lunch.

At some point in the form there will be an opportunity for you to put the meaty stuff in, the stuff that proves that you are the right person for the job. Here's where the reading you did about the job or person specification starts to pay off. They've given you great big clues as to exactly what they want from you. This bit is well worth writing out and revising a couple of times to get it absolutely right before you commit it irrevocably to the application form.

They don't just want you to regurgitate what it says in the specification, though. The key word is 'demonstrate'. Often the form will say just that: 'How would you demonstrate . . .' followed by whatever it is that they require you to demonstrate. Just writing 'I have an holistic approach to needs-based pastoral issues' won't do. You need to show that you understand what they're on about and then come up with examples. Preferably based on your experiences in a previous job. Sometimes you'll find a footnote at these parts saying something like 'Continue on a separate sheet if necessary.' Take them up on it. And if you're not sure whether you should or not, then call them up and ask them if it's okay.

This gives you an opportunity to wax lyrical (without waffling) about what a superb employee you would be. Personally I would also do that bit on my computer. It's easier to edit, it looks neater, it proves you're computer literate and you may be able to use it as a basis for future applications.

Don't be shy about singing your own praises. I know it's not very British to go about telling everyone how brilliant you are, but you're in a fierce competition here.

Better that you feel momentarily embarrassed than lose the job to someone with a keener sense of self-worth.

And speaking of what you're worth leads us neatly to the bit about 'Salary Expectations'. These are sometimes included on forms where the organization doesn't have a rigid wage structure and can be a little bit tricky. If you possibly can, it's a good idea to forestall this one. It can be a device to weed out unsuitable applicants. The recruiter takes a quick look at that box and bins all the ones that believe they're worth more than he can afford.

It's a far better thing to be discussing terms and conditions after you've made an impression at the interview, you have been offered the job and they're frothing at the mouth to employ you.

There may be cases where you feel you just can't dodge the issue, and you're going to have to use a little cunning. A favourite phrase deployed by those who'd rather wait before committing themselves runs along the lines of: 'I would expect to be paid a salary commensurate with my skills and responsibilities, but

GET REAL

Henry worked in a bank. He did something hideously hi-tech and complex, for which he was grotesquely well remunerated. But he hated it with every fibre of his being. He figured he'd got enough 'mad money' stashed to live comfortably for a couple of years and started to think about what it was he really wanted to do. He saw a vacancy for an office assistant in a private investigation company, and – perhaps befuddled from reading too many Raymond Chandler novels – called and got them to send out an application form. Under 'Current Salary' he simply put 'Vast'. Under 'Salary Expectations' he put 'Will work for food.' He got an interview purely because the company were amused and intrigued by his statements. At the interview it transpired that, in fact, they had been thinking about expanding into the area of financial investigations. Henry's banking background and computing expertise secured him a post as a trainee investigator.

am open to negotiation.' It kind of says, 'Look, don't take the mickey, and neither will I.' Another way to approach this one is to do a little research – you'll be pretty good at that by now. Find out what the top whack is for the job, and the minimum you could expect. Then put those figures in the box as 'between £x and £xx'. Or say, 'I am looking for a package worth around £xxx per year.' That way, the employer may figure that he might be able to afford to pay you a little less but top up the wages with perks and benefits.

Although there are things that are pretty much standard in all application forms – and you'll learn how to deal with them as they pile up in your mail box – occasionally you'll see something that really does call for some head scratching. If that happens then there's nothing to stop you ringing up and asking for clarification. Once again, it's a great way to make a personal contact, and it may be that the form is ill conceived; by diplomatically drawing attention to that fact, you've done everyone a favour. Besides, it's much better that you know what's expected before you start, as opposed to filling the thing in and getting it all totally wrong.

The last thing I'd advise regarding the filling in of an application form is to wait before sending it off, if at all possible. Preferably overnight. Given the complexity of the things, you'll perhaps benefit from coming to it afresh the day after. You could even pass it over for someone else to give it the once-over for a second opinion.

GET TICKED OFF

- Look out for newspaper situations vacant sections that are updated daily on the Internet
- Never send an application form in after the closing date without checking first
- Always carefully read the application form and all accompanying literature if at all possible. Refrain from putting down salary details or expectations
- If in doubt about something on a form, then ring up and ask

GET THAT INTERVIEWER TO LIKE **Y**OU

If there's one part of job hunting that can be more horrible than the distressing application form, it's the ghastly job interview. There's loads of potential there to get yourself properly wound up. It's by no means the ideal way for either you or the employer to find stuff out about each other, but sadly we're stuck with the system and we have to learn how to play it. Like everything else in this book (and pretty much in life) the more you do, the better you'll get at it. So don't get too annoyed with yourself if you get it a bit wrong the first couple of times.

With that in mind, it is sometimes suggested that if you're worried or inexperienced when it comes to interviews, you should try putting yourself through a couple, just for the experience. In other words, apply for jobs that you don't really want so that you can get some practice in. It may seem a little drastic, and it certainly wouldn't work for everyone, but it has evidently proved worthwhile for some people.

Whether you're attending an interview for real or purely as a rehearsal, the first thing that's obviously got to happen is that you hear you've actually got the thing. And this is where you need to start thinking straight away.

When the news arrives on your doorstep or answering machine, you'll naturally be in some state of high excitement. But you need to stay on your toes and after you've concluded the appropriate celebrations, get some thinking and planning done.

First off, you need to make sure you can attend the interview on the day and at the time you've been asked to attend. Of course you want to say 'Yes' and be prepared to shift heaven and earth to ensure you'll be there. Realistically though, there'll be occasions when there's some kind of difficulty. That's going to be particularly true for those of you who already have a job and need to ensure that you can get the time off work. You're potentially between a rock and a hard place, aren't you? Especially if your job search is being conducted with all the due diligence that results in a raft of interviews.

Only you know the best way to approach your

current employer, but if they don't know you're looking elsewhere – and you're starting to run out of excuses involving rotten teeth, sick grannies or dead dogs – then it may be best to come clean. As far as the prospective employer is concerned, you need to judge who needs whom the most. If you figure this is a job there'll be stiff competition for, you really should be there when they want you.

If you absolutely, positively have to break the engagement and reschedule, then just make sure that you give them a good reason. Current work commitments or another job interview should buy you some understanding and a possible date change.

If there's no problem and you can make the interview, then you need to let them know with all due haste. In the event that you got a letter informing you of the details, then use belt and braces. Call up immediately to confirm and then send a letter or e-mail. Not only does this make double certain that you're scheduled in, but the writing of a confirmation letter is a courtesy that apparently very few candidates bother with. Which is good for you, because you'll do it, taking the opportunity to show that you are an organized and professional person who would make an exceptional employee.

Having confirmed the interview, there is a bunch of practical stuff that you will need to know. And it's best asked over the phone with a little checklist in front of you. To save you the time and trouble of producing that list, here's one to copy:

• Where are you?
• Where's the nearest public transport stop?
• Is there car parking space?
• Could you send me a map?
• How long will the interview last?
• Do I get any travel expenses (overnight too, if it's a long way away)?
• Do I need to bring anything with me?

Hopefully, much of that information will be in your confirmation letter, which leaves you with the time to ask some rather more searching questions. Ones that are designed to give you a vital edge over the other candidates for the job.

Open up with a fairly basic one. 'What form will the interview take?' is a pretty useful question. It might give you a better mental picture of what to expect – let you know how many people will be interviewing you, for example, or whether or not there'll be any tests. It may also lead to information on the kind of questions you can expect, or give you an idea of the things you'll be expected to know. 'Is there anything else I need to know?' can also be a good one. If you've built a good rapport with the person you're speaking to, it might even lead to a revelation that the other candidates aren't privy to.

The best question ever in the history of asking questions in these circumstances is, 'Would it be okay if I spent some time at the company learning more about what you do?' It may even be worth asking if you can take a whole day there, shadowing someone who is doing the job you're after. You may get knocked back on this one, but it's well worth finding out, because on the occasions they give you the nod, you'll be able to get some really high-quality research in. Not only will you have the advantage of knowing more when it comes to the interview, but you'll also ascertain what kind of place it is to work in – thereby clarifying if you really want the job. And you'll probably get some valuable networking in, making potential allies and contacts for the future.

Once you've found out all you can from the person you spoke to, it's time for the real research to kick in. Go back to all the stuff you did initially (and, of course, kept on file). Revisit all those websites to see if anything new has pitched up. Call your personal contacts to see if they can shed any light on what might be required at the interview. Study the original advertisement and job specification again. Even if you've not been given the opportunity to spend a day at the organization, pay them a visit anyway. Not only will you then know where they are and how best to get there, but you could spot some potentially useful stuff. If you notice everyone goes to the same place after work or at lunchtime, follow them in. Eavesdrop. Clock how happy they are in their work. How busy they seem. Even the way they're dressed can be useful knowledge when it comes to deciding what to wear for the interview.

The day before the interview is when it really starts. Give yourself a quick refresher course on all the information you've gathered, then sit down and start thinking about what you're actually going to say in the interview. Then think about the answers to the questions you might be asked. We'll jump the gun a little here and start talking about those questions.

If you're serious about your job hunting, at least enough to have acquired this book, the chances are that you've also invested in a copy of one of those tomes called something like 'Every Answer To Every Interview Question Ever'. Take it back to the shop right now and ask for a refund. Or give it to a charity shop if you're feeling generous. Here's the deal. There's no way that you can memorize all those questions. Even if you could, the interviewer is not going to ask them all. They might even ask questions that aren't in the book.

Let's be honest here. There are going to be three distinctly different types of interviewer – and for your delectation, here's the by-now-obligatory acronymic mnemonic to study and learn:

• PROFESSIONAL
• IDIOT
• GIT

In reverse order then. The Git is the one that you probably think you're going to get, but in reality is hardly ever there. He – it is invariably a bloke – can be subdivided into the Pompous Git and the Ignorant Git. The PG will be asking questions designed to embarrass you, trip you up, catch you out and generally make you miserable. In the unlikely event that you get one of these, then you perhaps have to ask yourself 'Do I really want to work for this man? Or in a culture that encourages such behaviour?'

The same thing goes when it comes to working for the Ignorant Git. This time he's going to be asking you questions he really shouldn't be asking, perhaps based on his own small-minded prejudices. Here's a list of the kind of questions no one should ever ask you at an interview:

- What's your religion?
- What's your marital status?
- Are you gay?
- Are you courting?
- Do you live with anyone?
- Do you have any kids?
- Are you pregnant?
- Do you plan to have any kids?
- What does your spouse do?

It's actually against the law to ask many of the above, and if you seriously believe that a line of questioning at in interview is designed to discriminate against you on the grounds of gender, race or sexual orientation, then make like the homesick shepherd and get the flock out of there. Even if you take the job, you can rest assured that the harassment won't stop there.

The Idiot Class of interviewer is, unfortunately, a

little more prevalent. They usually don't mean to be an idiot, and it may well be that in every other respect they're a consummate and skilful professional. The trouble is that they have either given no thought to the questions they're going to be asking, or they're as stressed about the whole process as you are.

You're most likely to encounter the Idiot Class in a smaller outfit, where they just don't have the resources to justify a full-time personnel officer. To a certain extent you can take over the interview. The Idiot will be pleased because they don't have to struggle on ineptly, and you have a golden opportunity to ensure that you get across the information about yourself that is really vital. Just to give you one small example:

IDIOT: *I see you . . . umm . . . worked at St Patricia's as a vicar. How long were you there?*

YOU: *Three years.*

IDIOT: *Oh.*

SFX: *NOTHING. IN FACT, DEAFENING SILENCE FOR A WHOLE MINUTE.*

In those circumstances, you could try and lead the interview yourself, perhaps along something like the following lines:

IDIOT: *I see you . . . umm . . . worked at St Patricia's as a vicar. How long were you there?*

YOU: *Three years.*

IDIOT: *Oh.*

YOU: *For me it was one of the most productive three years of my career, to be honest. I learned so much about jumble sales I became one of the top organizers in the diocese. I also managed to convert quite a lot of sinners in that period, with very few backsliders.*

SFX: *BIG SIGH OF RELIEF FROM IDIOT AS HE REALIZES THAT YOU ARE GOING TO DO MOST OF THE WORK.*

The best kind of interview questions, and increasingly the most likely, are those that will be put to you by a fully trained personnel officer or human resources manager. Their job is to find out certain things about you as best they can. And in order to do that they'll have a list of questions. You do your bit by answering them in such a way that they get what they want. And what do they want? They basically want to know one of the following Famous Five:

1. Do you work hard?
2. Are you honest?
3. Are you clever?
4. Will you fit in here?
5. Can you do the job?

There will still be a huge variation in the way their questions are phrased. But at the end of the day they are looking for the same answers. So all you have to do is listen to the questions and work out which of the answers you prepared earlier is appropriate. So, for example, when someone asks that old recruiter's chestnut 'Where do you see yourself in five years?' they're hoping to find out numbers Four and Five.

Everybody would be a whole lot happier if they could just ask the Famous Five listed above outright and you could answer them all with an emphatic 'Yes.' But as no one is ever going to answer 'No', and because the interviewer wants to see a fully rounded answer that proves what you claim, the questions are going to be dressed up a little.

This puts the onus on you to dress up the answers so that you get across the message you want. If you're asked 'Where do you see yourself in five years?' and you figure that they're looking for the answer to number Four, then you can't just say 'Working with you guys and doing very nicely at it.' You need to reassure them in some way, perhaps show some evidence. Maybe something like this:

'Well, from what I've learned about this company so far, and from talking to the people here, I could imagine myself getting involved on a long-term basis. I was at my last place for six years, and would've been happy to carry on there, if I hadn't been made redundant.'

Which incidentally also answers, without prompting, that other old favourite – 'Why did you leave your last job?' It's pretty much guaranteed that you'll get that one, so give it some thought. If you think you're going to struggle with it because you were sacked, then you have to decide whether to come clean or not. Just remember that if you lie or bend the truth, you may well be in trouble if the new employer checks it out. You might decide that the best way to handle it is to own up and then elaborate on how much of a changed person you are.

You should also never say that you left your last job because your boss or colleagues were a bunch of idiots/crooks/scumbags. In fact, at no point during an interview should you take the opportunity to wade in and air grievances about former employers and colleagues. People see it as hugely unprofessional and it casts a big shadow over your integrity and discretion.

If you have had trouble getting along with someone in your previous or current job, and that's one of the reasons you're looking for a change, then be diplomatic. If you're being pushed on it then you could acknowledge that you had your differences perhaps, but that this is unusual because normally you get on

GET IN TOUCH The Equal Opportunities Commission is the place to go for information on your rights in the workplace, including those of an interviewee. They have a really good website at www.eoc.org.uk. If you're concerned that you may have been discriminated against in any way, you can check your facts there. And if you're convinced of the worst, the EOC will give you advice and fight your corner. Details of their offices in England, Wales and Scotland are listed on the home page.

really well with everyone. Stress into the bargain that in no way did the conflict have any effect on the quality of your work.

Let's reiterate here that the key is in the preparation. Keep the Famous Five 'real' questions in the forefront of your mind and spend some time thinking about them. Rehearse them with a friend or member of your family. We'll look later on at some tips on how to answer those questions under interview conditions.

The day before the interview is also the best time to

get all those other things sorted out. The sort of things you just know will go wrong if you leave them to the day. We're talking about checking public transport times, making sure your shirt is ironed, locating all the vital paperwork, anything else that you may have to take with you.

This is a good time to talk about appearance. What you should wear and how you should look for an interview. I hate this part. I have absolutely no right to tell you what to wear. But it seems that it's still a hot issue out there in the job-seeking world. Evidently there are employers who will put a big black mark against your name because you wear big dangly earrings or a pair of Laurel and Hardy socks. It's entirely up to you how you dress or groom yourself for an interview, or at any other time. Presumably, if you're not prepared to compromise your everyday look in the interests of getting a job, then one can only conclude that you don't really want that job in the first place.

However, if you are comfortable with the notion of dressing for the occasion, then there's a couple of things you might want to bear in mind. Even if you are going for a job where what you wear may not be of paramount importance, the fact that you make an effort does indicate to the interviewer that you are showing some respect for them and the situation. And being smart can't possibly do any harm when it comes to making an impact.

One oft-quoted example of relevance here is of the laid-back creative guys at Apple Mac computers who wanted to do a deal with the big suits at IBM computers. When it came to the initial meeting they put on their best whistles, combed their hair and gave their shoes a bit of a polish. Only to find when they arrived that the IBM straights – in deference to Apple Mac culture – had pitched up in jeans and trainers. Both parties had shown that they were prepared to fit in with the other's lifestyle, and that sent out a positive signal for their proposed business dealings.

There's also the not-to-be-underestimated feelgood factor. Looking the business will make you feel the business. If you look good and feel good, that will communicate itself to the interviewer, who will see you in an exponentially good light.

Look, if you are worried about how you should dress for an interview – and you're thinking 'Blimey this book's not much help' – then there are a couple of practical steps you can take. You could simply ring up and ask. If you've been doing your networking with any degree of success, you'll probably be on friendly enough terms with someone to have an informal chat by now. And as I pointed out earlier, you could always hang around the gaff as people come and go, scoping what they wear.

On the big day itself, you need a final run through your prepared answers and you need to leave the house dead early. Hopefully you've taken the previous advice and had a trial run so that you can get to grips with where the place is and how to get there. Even so, we all fall victim to time, circumstance and the vagaries of a creaky transport network. Far better to be hanging around for a half-hour than be even thirty seconds late. Or rushing in all hot and bothered,

GET REAL Michael writes books. You might even have read some of them. His biography of 1980s popular beat combo The Smiths and his history of Factory Records are well worth a look. He and I both would tell you that writing books can be a far from lucrative career. Usually you need some sort of back-up for the frequent periods inbetween publishers' whims. Faced with one of those lean periods, Michael embarked on a series of job interviews. He's not what you'd call a natural tie wearer – in fact, the only tie he owned was the one they supplied with his membership for Lancashire Cricket Club. So he wore that. Some interviewers, of course, never even noticed it, but fellow cricket enthusiasts would clock it immediately. In due course he was interviewed by a fellow member of the LCC, who engaged him in animated debate. They got on famously and Michael was hired to write for the guy's magazines.

flustered, dishevelled and ill prepared. Because that would mean making a bad entrance. And probably about half the battle with interviews is about making a good entrance.

We don't mean hiring a brass band to play a fanfare as you strut through the door like Robbie Williams picking up his Ivor Novello award. We mean walking in and presenting yourself in such a way that the interviewer or interviewers immediately relax, confident that they've found someone who at least looks like they might be able to do the job.

Apparently, there is an 'effect' that some people create at interviews, called the 'halo effect'. Some researchers looked into it, and – surprise, surprise – they discovered that first impressions count; that a candidate for a job is assessed from the moment that they walk through the door and if they make a favourable impression in the first thirty seconds or so, then that impression sticks. Likewise, if the instant impression you make is not a good one, then no matter how well you do in the rest of the interview, they're never going to hire you.

So, picture the interviewer sitting there, waiting for you. You open the door. They look at you. In the time it takes for you to sit down you've got to acquire a nice shiny halo. How are you going to do it?

The very process of thinking it through like that will help you. By getting that picture fixed in your head and acknowledging the fact that the first thirty seconds constitute make-or-break time, you'll be better equipped to deal with the situation. Try memorizing this acronymic mnemonic:

- Appearance
- Smile
- Handshake
- Eye Contact
- Sitting Right

See, it spells ASHES. The last one should be Body Language really, but that would spell ASHEB. Which wouldn't make sense. So let's run through them. Check your **Appearance** before you go in. It's another good reason to get there early – so you can give yourself the once-over in the mirror. Not much would be worse than realizing your flies were undone as you walked through the door. Evidently another bunch of researchers came up with research that shows people tend to look at your shoes and your fingernails as part of their instant evaluation process. I don't. But then I don't **Smile** much either. Be careful with this one. Grinning like an idiot won't do you many favours. Practise a good, friendly, professional smile in the mirror, maybe. Or take advice from someone who loves you on just how effective a smile you have.

The **Handshake** can also be practised. It seems it should be firm, but not painful. Under the rules of the 'halo effect' a limp or sweaty handshake would almost certainly undermine your instant aura of general saintliness. **Eye Contact** is important too. So make it. We've all encountered people who won't meet our gaze as we speak to them. Even if we give them the benefit of the doubt and put them down as shy – as opposed to shifty – it makes conversation unnerving and difficult.

And finally **Sitting Right**, or **Body Language**. There's been some hefty volumes written on this subject. My brother reads a load of that kind of stuff, and sometimes I think he's so busy trying to remember all the various rules of engagement, he forgets what he's actually there for. My advice would be to practise being in an interview situation with someone else and get them to point out anything that they feel is off-putting or looks bad. I evidently have a disconcerting habit of pursing my lips in a way that makes me look like a lecherous Tweety Pie when I'm concentrating. So in a formal interview-type situation, I make an effort to keep my lips in a straight line.

So there you are, you've ASHED and you're waiting for questions. You've run through the potential answers several times by now, so it's pretty much all in your head, but that first question comes and your head mysteriously empties. It could happen. And at some point, it most likely will. Don't panic. It sounds easy for me to say that, but it really is the best advice. Take this on board too: unless you're being interviewed by one of the aforementioned Gits, then the interviewer will have every sympathy with your plight. In the case of an Idiot, they probably feel as bad as you do.

So, take a moment to steady yourself, and then explain to the interviewer what's going on. Try saying something like, 'I'm sorry, I get a little nervous in interviews sometimes.' Or, 'Could you bear with me a second, I'm not used to this and I think my nerves got the better of me.' If you're being interviewed by the Professional, they'll quickly take that in their stride and do everything they can to put you at ease.

Once you start talking you'll find it all comes flooding back to you, and from then on it's just a case of listening carefully to the questions, sussing out which of the Famous Five they're really asking and then giving the answer they want. Don't be afraid to take a moment to think about a question before you answer it. A thoughtful and considered employee is a good one. Don't be afraid, either, to politely ask someone to repeat a question if you don't get it the first time. It's better to understand fully what you're being asked than to ramble on like an idiot about something else entirely.

Toward the end of the interview it's now customary to be asked, 'Is there anything you'd like to ask us?' It's perfectly acceptable to say, 'No I think you've covered everything.' Provided they have, of course. A rather radical question you could ask – if you think you'd get away with it – is 'Do you think I'll get the job?' It's worth a try sometimes. And here's an illustration of why. Because I'm a dumb klutz who one week before a deadline turns into a Super Dumb Klutz, I locked myself out of my house yesterday. Phil, the locksmith who came to help me out, told me he'd just started working for his company. At the interview he'd noticed that the boss – with whom he had struck up a rapport – bore a striking resemblance to Tom Baker, the former Doctor Who actor. At the end of the interview, Phil was asked if he wanted to ask anything. He replied, 'Just two things. Have I got the job, and do I need my own Sonic Screwdriver?' The boss laughed, and Phil was hired there and then. Use your judgement, obviously, but I think Phil's experience shows there are times when you can let your personality show through to good effect.

Even if you don't ask outright whether you got the job or not, you do need to know what happens next. A Professional will volunteer that information, but you may have to winkle it out of the Idiot. I don't know what happens with the Git. I'm sure you can think of some suitable suggestion involving the job and some lower part of his anatomy.

When the thing is over, you've left the room and had the chance to reflect on how it went, there's every chance you'll be a little disappointed with your performance. That's only natural. Especially in the early days, when you haven't done too many interviews. Don't worry about it too much. Have a think about where you went wrong and make sure you get it right next time. You could also turn that negative into a positive by writing a follow-up letter.

Some recruitment experts recommend writing a follow-up letter or e-mail after every interview. I'm not too sure about how productive that is. It is considered good manners, but may also be construed as a bit crawly. However, if you have something positive to put in there, then you should definitely go for it. Here's an example:

Dear Your Bishopness,

Thank you for seeing me this afternoon. I was really impressed with St Patricia's and enjoyed meeting you and the scout master. As you probably noticed, I was a little nervous at first, and I realized when I got home that I perhaps hadn't explained myself fully on the subject of my jumble sale experience.

I didn't really mention that at St Simon's I organized seven jumble sales, all of which resulted in record takings, with no injuries to excited old ladies. I have also studied Bishop Bob Inchpenny's book *The Holistic Approach to Jumble* and have applied its principles to all of my jumble sales.

I hope this clarifies things, and I look forward to

hearing from you soon.

Yours etc.

The faster you get that off, the better. It can only create a good impression, and may even swing a few points in your favour. It's certainly unlikely to do your cause any harm.

If you don't get a job at a place, and you reckon you did all of the above, and made a pretty good show, then don't give up on that company. Ask for feedback. Use it, and stay in touch. You could say something along the following lines to them: 'Look, if I worked really hard on this specific area, what would be the chances of you considering me next time a vacancy came up?' For all you know it could have been a really close thing between you and the person who actually got the job.

The very, very worst thing about being a diligent job hunter is that sometimes you do everything you possibly can, as well as you can, and you still don't get a result. You do great research, diligently network, write a stunning CV, give cracking interviews, and it all comes to nothing. And that will happen. Maybe even a few times. And it stinks. And I feel really bad about it, but the very best words anyone can offe, is that you have to stick at it, and you will come good. Especially after you polish up your skills and gain confidence in your abilities.

GET TICKED OFF

- Check all details as soon as you get notification of an interview
- Write a confirmation letter or e-mail immediately
- Do all preparation the day before and turn up early
- Remember, ASHES: appearance, smile, handshake, eye contact, sit right
- Work out which of the famous five questions you're really being asked

If you want a job, you'll get one. And when you do, you can use this book as a doorstop. I do. Good luck.

USEFUL
INFORMATION

Useful websites & phone numbers

websites

www.ask.com

www.careers-uk.com

www.crimes-of-persuasion.com

www.employmentservice.gov.uk

www.eoc.org.uk

www.jobhunter.co.uk

www.jobline.co.uk

www.jobpilot.co.uk

www.jobs.co.uk

www.jobsearch.co.uk

www.jobsite.co.uk

www.jobsnetwork.co.uk

www.jobsunlimited.co.uk

www.monster.co.uk

www.thesite.org

phone numbers

Career Development Loans information line
0800 585 505

Consumer credit Counselling Service
0800 138 1111

Directory Enquiries
192

Employment Services
0845 606 0234

DTI employment agencies helpline
08459 555105

Learn Direct helpline
0800 100 900

Your rights at work

From the day you start, you are entitled to:

- A minimum wage of £4.10 an hour; £3.50 if you're under 21
- Payslips detailing gross pay, deductions and net pay
- Not to be unfairly dismissed for asserting your rights, raising health and safety issues or trade union activities
- Work no more than 48 hours per week
- Regular work breaks
- Time off for family emergencies
- Eighteen weeks' maternity leave
- Paid time off for antenatal appointments
- Not to be discriminated against on the grounds of sex, race or disability
- To be paid the same wages for doing work of equal value whether you are male or female

After two months you are entitled to:

- A copy of written terms and conditions of employment

After thirteen weeks you are entitled to:

- Four weeks' paid holiday a year

After twelve months you are entitled to:

- Parental leave for children under five
- Forty weeks' maternity leave

After two years you are entitled to:

- Redundancy pay

Do's and Don'ts at interviews

DON'T let your hair obscure your eyes. You need to be able to make eye contact. It looks like you're hiding behind it.

DON'T have a hairstyle that means you have to keep messing with it. It's distracting to the interviewer.

DON'T forget to shave. Stubble is trouble. Looks great on George Clooney. Looks like you haven't bothered to shave.

DON'T have spectacles patched up with wire, sticky-tape and matchsticks. Looks like you're not bothered about details. Make sure they're clean as well.

DON'T wear shades. Dark glasses render it impossible to make eye contact.

DON'T wear too many dark clothes. It looks too gloomy. So have some discreet colour splashed about. Trainee undertakers or hitmen can ignore this advice.

DON'T wear garish socks. Not just for interviews, but in life generally we would've thought.

DON'T wear jeans, and no trainers, no baseball caps, no sportswear. Come on, you'd do it to get into a fancy nightclub.

Brightly coloured hair is a no-no.

DO clean your teeth. And check in a mirror before you go in. Just in case bits of breakfast are hanging around between your teeth.

DO use some breath freshener or gum before you go in. But don't keep the gum in for the interview. Don't take it out and stick it behind your ear either.

DO keep those nails clean and short and tidy. It's another weird thing people look at as a test of character.

DO remember it will rain. So a raincoat, a hat and/or umbrella are all worth considering.

DO carry a bag. But not a plastic carrier bag from Cheapo Supastores. The recommendation is a small attaché case or leather folder. Don't have two bags if you're a woman. Put everything into one smart, slimline affair.

- DO leave all your other accoutrements, spare shoes, umbrella, coat, ski-mask in reception before you go into the interview. You don't want to be fumbling around with stuff while you're in there.

- DO make sure you look okay from the back as well. You don't want the skirt tucked into the knickers thing happening do you?

- DO watch out for the translucent. You don't want the knickers showing through the skirt thing happening do you? Trainee clip-joint hostesses can ignore this advice.

- DO wear a bra. And tights or stockings. No, fellas, you can definitely ignore that.

- DO ditch any badges, jewellery or insignia that affiliates you with any kind of religious, political or social group. You might just arouse some prejudice in an interviewer. Particularly horrible one that isn't it?

- DO have a hanky. In case you've got a cold, hayfever or allergies to slimy bigots. Tissues are not good. They get too snotty too quickly.

- DO have a bath. And use deodorant. Oh for crying out loud. Honestly, that's one of the top ten tips in the opinion of a lot of 'recruitment experts'.

Notes